CAIN

A Dramatic Mystery in Three Acts

CAIN

A Dramatic Mystery in Three Acts

By
Lord Byron

Translated into French Verse
and refuted in a series of Philosophical and Critical Remarks
Preceded by
a letter addressed to Lord Byron, upon the motives
and the purpose of this work

By

Fabre d'Olivet

Done into English by

Nayán Louise Redfield

כי שכעתים יקס קיז
So sevenfold shall be exalted Kain

Hermetica

San Rafael, Ca

Second, facsimile edition,
Hermetica, 2007
First edition, G.P. Putnam's Sons, 1923

For information, address:
Hermetica, P.O. Box 151011
San Rafael, California 94915, USA

Library of Congress Cataloging-in-Publication Data

Byron, George Gordon Byron, Baron, 1788–1824.
Cain: a dramatic mystery in three acts / by Lord Byron;
refuted in a series of philosophical and critical remarks preceded by
a letter addressed to Lord Byron, upon the motives and the
purpose of this work [by] Fabre d'Olivet; translated
by Nayán Redfield. — Reprint ed.

p. cm.
"First edition, G.P. Putnam's Sons, NY, 1923"—T.p. verso.
ISBN-13: 978-1-59731-202-8 (pbk.: alk. paper)
ISBN-13: 978-1-59731-208-0 (hardcover: alk. paper)
I. Fabre d'Olivet, Antoine, 1767–1825. II. Redfield, Nayán Louise.
III. Fabre d'Olivet, Antoine, 1767–1825. Lettre de Fabre d'Olivet
à Lord Byron exposant les motifs et le but de son
ouvrage sur Caïn. English. IV. Title.
PR4356.A1 2007
822'.7—dc22   2007027046

To

THE LIGHT SEEKERS

WHO HAVE REACHED THE STATION OF THE

"EYE SINGLE"

HAVING THE FACULTY OF DIFFERENTIATING DISCRIMINATION

I CONFIDENTLY OFFER THIS

VOLUME

(*St. Luke xi, 34*)

TRANSLATOR'S FOREWORD

AT the moment when *Cain*, the dramatic mystery of Lord Byron, fell into the hands of Fabre d'Olivet, he was absorbed in a Commentary upon his new translation of the Cosmogony of Moses. The admirable beauties of form in this poem did not conceal from him the "infernal perversity" of its substance. Therefore putting aside his serious studies he devoted himself for fifteen days to translating *Cain* into French, in order to place himself in a position to refute it and to prove that the foundation upon which Lord Byron had built his very beautiful work was utterly false. Taking the astonishing poem as the expression of Lord Byron's sentiments, Fabre d'Olivet was led to see in the *Dramatic Mystery of Cain*, "the statement of a doctrine that is injurious for you, dangerous for others, inadmissible for me and that it is my duty to combat."

Armed with the power of his colossal erudition, he has refuted this false doctrine and has shown that there exist two methods for writing history. The one is occupied with individuals and facts considered one after another; the other, applied for a long time by the ancients, treats only of the evolutions of the moral law, without concerning itself with individuals or with facts other than in their relations to this law.

The Mosaic Cosmogony of Fabre d'Olivet is derived in its entirety from the *Sepher* of Moses, and one should have read his translation of the *Beræshith* to comprehend how the esoteric ideas of the Egyptians upon the creation differ from the simple narratives of the exoteric translators of Moses, and are, instead, profoundly psycho-philosophical writings containing the chronicle of the human soul, its origin, phases of involution and evolution, and the means whereby it may ultimately reattain its origin.

In *Cain*, Fabre d'Olivet partly draws aside the veil, shedding new lights upon the Cosmogony of Moses, in defining Nahash, Adam, Eve, Cain and Abel in their esoteric relations. These proper names do not designate individuals, but principles, and the acceptation given them is rigorously and scientifically deduced from the esoteric roots of the Mosaic language. While unfolding some of the inner meaning of these words, he yet judiciously leaves other veils over many arcana. Swedenborg in his *Arcana Cælestia* writes, "If anyone could know how many arcana each particular verse contains, he would be perfectly astonished; for although there is but little evidence of their existence in the letter, they are too numerous ever to be explained."

Quoting from d'Olivet's letter to Lord Byron:

"Cain and Abel are the two primordial forces of elementary nature. These are the first two cosmogonic beings produced by Eve, when after a certain movement toward elementary nature, she has lost her name of *Aisha*, which designated the intellectual nature of Adam, to take that of Eve, which expresses no more than the material life of this universal being. It is in this material life that Cain and Abel took birth, and that their principles, which were in power of being from the origin of things, passed into action to produce all that which must in the future constitute that life.

"Cain can be conceived as the action of compressive force, and Abel as that of expansive force. These two actions, issues of the same source, are hostile from the moment of their birth, according to the manner by which everything exists in nature. They act incessantly the one upon the other, and seek reciprocally to dominate and to be reduced to their own nature. The compressive action, more energetic than the expansive action, always gains the ascendancy in the beginning; and overwhelming it, so to speak, compacts the universal substance upon which it acts, and gives existence to material forms that were not previously."

Fabre d'Olivet had found that what is called today the Hebraic tongue, is only a colourless simulation of the tongue of the mysteries, and that in finding again this mysterious language one would hold at last the key of all cosmogonies. Drawing upon the resources acquired by his exhaustive studies of Chinese, Sanskrit, Samaritan, Chaldaic, Syriac, Arabic, and Greek, he restored the tongue of the mysteries. In his *Hebraic Tongue Restored*, he established a grammar so lofty in its constituent principles, so meritorious, that it can be applied to nearly all known mother-tongues. He translated the first ten chapters of the Genesis of Moses; and of the three meanings which he had discovered in the words of this mysterious language, gave the second meaning, not wishing to profane the mysteries of the higher, or to remain in the exotericism of the grosser.

Stanislas de Guaita, in *Au Seuil du Mystère*, relates that "death struck the restorer of the Hebraic Tongue as he was preparing his Commentaries on the Cosmogony of Moses by way of indispensable complement to the most gigantic of his productions. It is assured that the precious manuscript is not lost. The critical remarks by Fabre d'Olivet in *Cain* (1823), the last work that he published, can supply the deficiency of his unpublished Commentaries in giving the intimate thought of this theosophist upon many points otherwise obscure. . . . He allows the limpid spirit to filtrate through the troubling denseness of the letter."

Percy Lund, writing in *The Seeker*, says:

"Orthodox scholarship, which runs in grooves, will be slow to take advantage of the insight and intellectual achievements of this isolated student, but those who have already accustomed themselves to search for deeper truths veiled in philosophical allegory will quickly recognize and avail themselves of the merits of his work. . . . Despite obvious counsel to the contrary, in direct contravention of innumerable veiled hints throughout mystic, hermetic, cryptic or arcane literature, the vast majority still persist in following the letter and ignoring the spirit, thereby inflicting upon themselves psychological suicide. . . . Within you and me Adam and Eve are generating Cain, Abel and Seth, and their offspring or seed. We are, or have within us also, the principles and faculties known as Noah, Abraham, Isaac, and Jacob. . . . Fabre d'Olivet has clearly demonstrated that the names in Genesis are not those of *persons*, but of metaphysical *principles* and *faculties* which are gradually developed one from the other by a process allied to that of chemical combination, and most appropriately symbolized by the physical activities of marriage and childbirth. . . . We shall see also the gradual development of a system of *geographical* symbolism, wherein the place-names indicate the environment or outlook or "house" of the soul at that particular level."

With this understanding of Fabre d'Olivet's viewpoint one can appreciate his feeling for the necessity of refuting Lord Byron's *Cain*. Not only does he indicate the falsity of the principles therein propagated, but he also shows up its dramatical, psychological, and moral untruths. He reveals himself as eminent scholar as well as mystic.

Lord Byron's laconic reply to the brilliant refutation of his *Cain* is said to have been that he was "a poet and not a metaphysician."

NAYÁN LOUISE REDFIELD.

Hartford, Conn.,
July, 1923.

CONTENTS

Letter to Lord Byron

LETTER TO LORD BYRON

My Lord,

The brilliant poetical reputation that you have acquired, the rumour of which has covered Europe, could not fail to reach me. Although absorbed in literary labours of another nature than yours, I could not remain so distant from the beaux-arts that I loved and cultivated in my youth, as not to know that Lord Byron was placed in the first rank of the English poets and that he reached out, by the force and originality of his genius, to seize the sceptre of poetry among the poets of all the European nations. Nevertheless, despite this *éclat*, the transitory and indirect lights of which had often come to strike me in the inner court of my retreat, I admit that I was unacquainted with any of your works; I regarded them as purely poetical, and supposed to find in them, as one finds in modern poetry generally, only literary forms more or less pretentious or more or less affected by a sort of research and labour in which I am no longer interested.

I left the poetical career at the moment when you entered, my lord. I withdrew wearied with the perpetual descriptions that I had heard. I judged that there were enough of them upon the sun and the moon, the flowers of spring, the fruits of autumn, the calm of hamlets, the care of flocks, glory and victory, loves and beautiful days, arms and alarms, tempests of seas, sons of the desert and a thousand other beautiful things that rhyme incessantly introduces for the greater variety of poetry. I was hardly less bored, I also admit, with the ever repeated depictions of the same passions, ever expressed in the same terms. Our poets, forced to link together the same rhymes and to introduce the same pictures, finished by persuading me that modern poetry, ready to be buried under its own productions, could only drag itself out from this oppression by the effect of a sufficiently great effort. I believed that, above all for French poetry, the only one that I had at all cultivated, this effort consisted principally in throwing off the yoke of rhyme; and I made in this regard some preparatory works, of which I will spare you the details. My design in writing you this letter is not simply to converse with you on poetry, this subject being infinitely more familiar to you than to me. Europe ought to receive lessons from you, rather than to pretend to give them to you by the agency of any poet whatsoever. But to arrive at the important subject that has caused me to take up my pen, it is necessary first to touch upon the reasons that have led me to do so. The one that I indicate now is one of the least. I shall show you later the more powerful and decisive ones.

The works of which I have just spoken, my lord, and which tended to give to French poetry a form of versification long since adopted by the poets of other European nations, and above all by the English, when presented to the *Institut de France*, did not obtain its assent. Concerning my first attempts, the *Académie Française*, having offered a prize on the question as to whether the French tongue is or is not susceptible of receiving unrhymed verse, did not judge that there was a single Frenchman capable of solving the question. To the general astonishment of the poetic world, it awarded the prize to a certain Italian abbé, perhaps Corsican, whose name I have forgotten. This abbé had the extreme pleasure of coming from Naples to Paris, on purpose to inform us, to the eternal shame of our most able grammarians, that our tongue lacked rhythmic prosody and that it was condemned by its native monotony to possess only rhymed verses.

Because of the affront that I received, I can scarcely tell whether as Frenchman or as poet, I was somewhat shocked at this decree; and I allowed myself to doubt the infallibility of a tribunal which, in a question wholly French, that a Frenchman alone could decide, wilfully awarded the prize to an Italian. Be that as it may, I saw that it was necessary to renounce for the time the project—perhaps rash—that I had formed; to abandon poetry and await the appeal that I believed time would inevitably lodge against the judgment carried by the *Institut de France*, on the more than doubted report of an Italian advocate, with regard to the supposed inaptitude of our tongue ever to receive rhythmic prosody.

In this situation, while I was occupied with very serious studies, and principally with a commentary upon a new translation of the *Cosmogony of Moses* that I had published several years ago, a hazard that I shall consider as happy if you will give some attention, my lord, caused to fall into my hands your poem of *Cain*. The subject, which is necessarily found in the line of my present labours, struck me; and your name having given me the certitude that it must be treated with grandeur, led me to read it. To speak of the effect that its reading caused in me is a thing impossible for the moment. You will judge of it in considering the resolution that has been the consequence.

That this work is a very beautiful piece of poetry is assuredly beyond doubt. I know of nothing in the same style which might be compared with it. You are, my lord, a poet directly inspired and I do not believe that since Homer a single one has been able to aspire to the same prerogative. But I cannot apply to you the idea of Plato, and believe, according to this philosopher, that you can, like the poets he cites, yield to a blind inspiration, and moved by a certain enthusiasm, say things that you do not understand. I am therefore obliged to take your astonishing poem as the expression of your sentiments, and find myself led to see in the *Dramatic Mystery of Cain*, the statement of a doctrine that is injurious for you, dangerous for others, inadmissible for me, and that it is my duty to combat.

I hope that you will be in nowise offended. If your poem were not one of the most extraordinary productions of our century, if even it were remarkable only from the side of poetry, I should not concern myself with it. You have done other works which contain, I am told, beauties of the first order; and I am not surprised. You can only give out that which is in you,—a very beautiful and very strong poetry. One accuses you of depicting with too much verity the stormy passions which upset the heart of man, and the frightful calamities which afflict nature. These things are unfortunately only too common. The choice that you make depends upon yourself, and I do not see who would have the right to find fault with you.

> There is no serpent, or any odious monster
> Which, by art of imitation, may not please the eye.

But, it is said, the picture that you draw with so much verity of the vices and the terrible catastrophes of which human life offers a spectacle, affects weak imaginations, troubles them and tends to lead them astray. This I do not believe. Since these things are in nature, it is well that man should know them, whether to stifle the causes in himself, or to avoid the effects in others. It is not in order to frighten mariners or to make them love shipwrecks that one charts the reefs with which the seas are strewn, and that one describes the storms which stir up the waves; but in order to enlighten their inexperience, to warn them against false security and teach them to foresee or to surmount the obstacles of navigation. Thus, therefore, I find everything useful, whether one describe the irregularities of Don Juan or of Sardanapalus, or the admirable actions of Socrates or of Titus. If you had applied your poetry only to depict human individuals, of whatever nature they might be, I should no doubt have admired your talent from the moment it had come to my knowledge; but, considering your works as wholly foreign to my occupations, I should not have applied myself to translate them in order to combat them. Furthermore, if anyone had come to me to say, as has happened several times, that you were believed to be inspired by Satan himself, on account of the force and the verity that you put into portraying infernal characters and satanic works, I should have smiled at praise so extraordinary; but I should not have considered as praise an accusation which is as strange as it is ridiculous.

You may ask me then, why I have put so much earnestness into translating your *Mystery of Cain* and so much importance on refuting it. This is why, my lord. It is that those you have put in the scene are not human individuals, but cosmogonic principles; neither have you exposed particular actions or chance opinions, but you have travestied universal acts and fundamental dogmas. You have not taken from a positive history the positive facts that you have told, and from which you have drawn the most redoubtable inductions, but from a sacred book, the original text of which is unknown to you, and which you do not understand. I pray you not to be scandalized by what I have just said; for, as Boileau said somewhat amusingly, "Qu'on peut être honnête homme et mal faire les vers," I say with more truth still, and without the least pleasantry, that not only can one make good verse, but one can even be the foremost poet of the world and the most distinguished man, without understanding Hebrew.

As it may be possible, my lord, that the course of your studies has never brought you to this subject, or that, having brought you to it, you have let the traces of it be effaced by other occupations or other ideas, I crave permission to engage you here a moment.

The facts upon which your *Dramatic Mystery of Cain* repose, are, as you undoubtedly believe, contained in the first chapters of a holy book called the *Bible*. But the very title of the *Bible*, which signifies the *Book* in Greek, and which consequently indicates a Greek origin, announces that it is

only a version of a much more ancient work; it is that of the
prophet of the Hebrews, Moses; and it contains the cosmogony of that celebrated man, and his sacred doctrine.
Now, the work of Moses exists in the original; it is written
in Hebrew, under the title of *Sepher;* and the first chapters,
in which are found the cosmogonic acts that you, with the
Greek translators, have taken for historical facts, bear, in
the original, the name of *Bœreshith*, which has been interpreted by that of *Genesis*.

But if there exists an original of the *Bible*, called *Sepher*,
as is very certain, it is evident that this original should have
the authority of preference to the copy.   Before stating as a
fact that such or such thing was said by Moses and is found
in the sacred book of the Hebrews, and above all before
taking from it consequences so formidable as those you have
taken, it must be proved not only that these things are in the
Bible, but also that they are in the *Sepher;* that is to say, in
the original text of which the *Bible* is only a version.   It is
true that to undertake such a thing, it is necessary to understand Hebrew,—the original Hebrew, such as Moses understood,—not the Hebrew of the schools, which is only an
apograph of the Greek version, since all the Hebrew diction-
aries that we possess are formed upon this version.   For,
consider attentively, my lord, that as the Greek version of
the *Sepher* has served as type to give a signification to all the
Hebrew words that enter into the composition of this sacred
book, the Hebrew lexicons can never give us, whether in
Greek or in Latin, other than the same meaning given by
this version.   Therefore to know the Hebrew of the schools
is only to know the Greek version and to know the Greek

version is only to know the Hebrew of the schools, that is to say, the Hebrew of that same version, which can be very different from the Hebrew of Moses; and indeed it is very much so. This a vicious circle from which it is difficult to escape.

The savants who occupy themselves with this matter have conceived a dismay; a dismay so much the greater, because they have seen and are unable to doubt that the Hebraic tongue, that in which Moses wrote, altered by the successive revolutions to which the Hebrew people were prey during nearly a thousand years, was irrevocably lost at the epoch of the Babylonian captivity. Thus it no longer existed when, some four hundred years afterwards, the king of Egypt, Ptolemy, son of Lagus, raised in Alexandria that superb library which he confided to the keeping of Demetrius of Phalerus. Conceiving the plan of enriching this monument with all the most precious literature of the peoples, he ordered the translation into Greek of the *Sepher* of Moses, an exemplar of which he had received from the sovereign pontiff Eleazar. The difficulty of finding Jews in Alexandria who might understand a tongue lost for so great a number of years was not the only barrier that opposed itself to the execution of the king's plans. The Essenes, to whom Demetrius addressed himself, the only ones in a position to respond to his hope, found in their worship an obstacle insurmountable to his desires. They could not without crime violate the mystery of the holy book. A revered tradition menaced with the wrath of God the one who would dare to explain the text to strangers. Pressed between the religious law that forbade the communication of divine mysteries and the authority of the prince who ordered them to translate the

Sepher, it appears that these sectarians took a somewhat clever bias. Possessors of the oral tradition preserved since Moses, they knew that the text of the *Sepher* was constructed in such a manner as to present, in the *Bæreshith*, three meanings perfectly distinct, although closely linked together: the first proper, the second figurative, the third hieroglyphic. Under this triple relation, the holy book was compared by them to the universe and to man, and was composed equally of body, soul and spirit. By the body of the book they understood the gross and material sense; by the spirit and soul, the spiritual and mysterious sense, lost to the vulgar. In giving what they called the body of the *Sepher*, they obeyed the civil authority, and in retaining the spirit, their conscience. Thus they made a version which was neither wholly exact, nor completely inexact. Of the three parts of one same thing, they gave one, that which served as covering for the other two, and which could not compromise the secrets that they had sworn to guard inviolably.

What I have just explained to you here in a concise manner, I have already explained with great detail in a work that I published more than six years ago, entitled *La Langue Hébraïque Restituée*,[1] of which five hundred exemplars already circulate in the savant world; this is sufficient to show that a work of such nature is known and appreciated. It is there that I have brought together the proofs of what I have just told you; and there I have shown, upheld by the foundation of a somewhat large erudition and a somewhat deep knowledge of the tongues of the Orient, "that the Hebraic tongue, already corrupted by a rude people and brought

[1] *The Hebraic Tongue Restored*, Fabre d'Olivet. Pub. Putnam, N. Y.

down from its original intellectual state, to its most material elements, was entirely lost after the captivity of Babylon." It is an historical fact which it is impossible to doubt, whatever skepticism one may have. The *Bible* shows it; the *Talmud* affirms it; it is the sentiment of the most famous rabbis; Walton, author of the Prolegomena in the fine Polyglot of London, does not deny it; the best critic that has ever written on this matter, Richard Simon, never wearies of repeating it. Since my intention, my lord, is not to exhaust you with uncalled-for erudition, I would recommend this latter writer to you, if you judge fitting to verify my quotations. See, in this case, his *Critical History of the Old Testament.* B. I., ch. 8, 16 and 17.

Now this important fact being established, and long since known by the savants of all cults, Israelites, Christians and even Mussulmans, how can it be doubted that many among them have not undertaken to restore the Hebraic tongue, so as to penetrate by its means into the mysteries of a sacred book? This book is not only venerated because it serves as fundamental basis to the three most powerful cults of the earth, but is also respected for its antiquity, and very interesting in this regard alone. It is certain that many have made, at diverse times and among different nations, very great efforts to attain to this end. The savant Israelites and the Mussulmans of the fruitful centuries of the caliphs Al-Rashid, Al-Mamoun and Al-Mansor, were no doubt the first to succeed; but their success remained almost entirely unknown and circumscribed to themselves alone, on account of the prejudices of their cult which forbade them to divulge the truth. Several, nevertheless, made use of their learning to give impetus to science and advancement to the human mind. Such was, among the Mussulmans, the celebrated Aben-Roshi whom we name Averroës, who, in translating the works of Aristotle into Arabic for the first time, and in commenting on the Greek philosophy, changed the face of Europe. Into the midst of the darkness that covered it, he threw a light which, increasing gradually, brought back at last all the brilliance of the sciences that the ferocity of the barbarians had extinguished, and all the beauties of the arts that their destructive sword had annihilated. The learned Israelites often were satisfied to enclose their doctrine in obscure books that were called kabalistic, on account of a certain oral tradition, named *Kabala* in their idiom. As I have said in speaking of the Essenes, the oral tradition was traced back to Moses and these Israelites claimed likewise to be the possessors of it. Among those who have made of this *Kabala* a use most serviceable to the sciences, should be cited, among the ancients, Hillel, the most illustrious of the editors of the sacred text after Esdras; and among the moderns, Maimonides and above all, Spinoza.

The latter, who is not at all well-known and is greatly disfigured by his interpreters, is certainly of the modern savants, the one who has contributed most to the development of learning. He occasioned violent shocks as much in the opinions of his own adherents as in those of his opponents. The men who have accused him of materialism and of atheism have understood nothing of the signification of these two terms. Spinoza is the most puissant unitarian that has appeared in the world. The axioms that he gave in favour of universal unity have not yet been overthrown.

You, my lord, as much as I can glimpse it in your *Cain*, the only work of yours that I know, are a puissant diarchist, that is to say, a promoter of the two principles. It has been said that you are an atheist, but this is the most absurd contradiction. You are perhaps more religious than the greater part of those who accuse you of atheism, without having the force to sound the depths of your own system. The sole point where you err, according to me, is in the confusion that you have made of the two principles you admit. But we shall have time to return to this subject in the remarks that I propose to make further on. Let us continue.

I said that the learned Israelites and Mussulmans were trained in the sure truth that the Hebraic tongue, already disfigured during the lapse of time which had unrolled between the mission of Moses and the captivity of Babylon, was entirely lost during this captivity; that they made frequent efforts to restore it, and to penetrate by its means into the sacred mysteries of the *Sepher*—efforts which, for several of them, were crowned with success. The Chaldaic, Syriac and Arabic tongues that they possessed gave them facilities for this which were lacking to the Christians of Europe. Among the Christians of Asia, and especially among those of Africa who were established in Egypt, were found many who at first enjoyed the same advantage. But the lights that they tried to diffuse were quickly extinguished by the fatal calamities that assailed the Roman Empire: the corruption that struck at its still poorly established foundations and the irruption of the Barbarians that shook its political edifice from top to bottom.

The European Christians having added to fanaticism,

for which the Jews were already much reproached, the savage intolerance of the Goths, were deprived of discernment and reflection. They refused to recognize as Christians those who, at the council of Nicea, admitted as they did, the dogmas of Christianism, and who, in the school of Alexandria that was raised as a sanctuary, had created all its rites. They treated as heretics those who claimed to any knowledge in those dark days of the reign of the Vandals, Herules and Franks, and derided the name of gnostics or of savants whom they were incapable of understanding or of enduring. At that time the celebrated Hypatia was massacred in the streets of Alexandria; the books of Origen were anathematized; and it was no longer remembered that to his master Ammonius Saccus was owed that admirable rite of the Catholic mass, which Luther condemned because he was not able to feel its mysterious beauties.

From that time down to this same Luther, who succeeded in consolidating in Christianism a reform already vainly attempted, I do not see that the Hebraic tongue was understood in its intimate genius by any Christian of distinction, —unless perhaps by Raymond Lully, who, impressed by the advantages that could be derived by comprehension of the holy book, made unbelievable efforts to have the study of Hebrew admitted into the universities, with that of Arabic and the other Oriental tongues. Before him, that is to say, before the middle of the thirteenth century, one hardly knew, notwithstanding the works executed by Saint Jerome at the end of the fourth century, that there existed an Hebraic tongue from which one could draw any help for the advancement of the Christian religion. The thousand years of darkness that had covered Europe were now beginning to give way to a faint dawn. Although one might possess a Latin *Vulgate*, the Greek *Bible* continued none the less to be the authority. Everything was brought back to this incorrect copy; it was consulted with the religious respect that was due only to the original; and even in the time of Saint Augustine, who said it expressly, one was completely ignorant of the fact that this original existed.

When, thanks to the efforts of Raymond Lully, the existence of this original was again perceived, prejudice in this regard was still so strong that Cardinal Ximines, printing in 1515 a *Polyglot* of Hebrew, Greek and Latin, placed the Latin between the Hebraic and the Greek versions and compared this *Bible*, thus ranged in three columns, to Jesus Christ between the two robbers; the Hebrew text, according to his sentiment, represented the wicked robber. Three centuries ago, and at the moment of the appearance of Luther, the original work of the prophet of the Hebrews was thus treated by a prince of the church.

Despite all the pains that Luther gave himself to understand Hebrew, this chief of the Reform never understood it; and this because the violence of his character, which bore him on to divide and to destroy, had nothing of calm sufficient to lead him to the comprehension of any mystery, or to the edification of any truth. He rejected several mysteries of Christianism under pretext that he did not understand them and that they were repugnant to reason. If he had dared to follow this first step that his audacious character made him undertake, he would have rejected, one after another, all the mysteries that he did not comprehend, even as Erasmus and Bayle have maliciously observed. Bayle proclaims in his caustic, concise style, that it is inconsistent with human reason to reject two things out of ten or twelve, when it is demonstrated that all the twelve are equally incomprehensible; and that it is necessary, either to reject all the twelve if one lacks the faith, or to admit all the twelve if one does not lack it. Faith, indeed, is not a thing that admits the more or the less, as cold or heat.

But Luther, as you very well know, my lord, prided himself on being the most consistent of men. He had that in common with Calvin, but he was better and more tolerant than his disciple. Nevertheless this bold innovator who rejected with audacity the authority of the sovereign pontiff, whom he had acknowledged in his office as member of the sacerdotal body; who released the monks, his colleagues, from their oaths in order to release himself from his; who abolished by his private authority the sacrifice of the mass; who rejected the dogma of the real presence in the sacrament of the Eucharist; who said all these things were contrary to justice and sane reason, admitted a host of others that the same justice and the same sane reason could have likewise contested and for which it was necessary to have faith. But since he had denied the authority of the church, and since he had ignored his supreme chief, who should be the regulator of this faith? To what should it be given? To what should it be refused? Was it not to be feared that it might be placed where it should not be placed and that it might not be placed where it should be? Luther, in order to extricate himself from this embarrassment, put down this fundamental axiom, "that the Scripture alone is and must be the rule of faith; and that every man of sane understanding, of just mind, becomes its legitimate interpreter after putting himself in condition so to be by study, or when God has deigned to grant him the intelligence."

Very well. You were, my lord, brought up in the Reformed religion, and I also. Both pupils in this doctrine, we can understand each other perfectly; and if I have nothing with which to reproach you as heretic, you need have no fear as to my orthodoxy.

Now let us see. You have chosen from the *Sepher* of Moses, from what Luther called the Scripture, a text; and you have paraphrased it in a poem, admirable from the standpoint of poetry, but from the standpoint of the inductions that you have drawn from it, erroneous to the highest degree. Find it fitting that I tell you this, my lord; you are strong enough in intelligence and genius to permit me to tell you the truth. I have tried to make it acceptable to you; do not repulse it at the first word; wait to read all that I have to say, then you can decide. I have translated your eighteen hundred lines with animation, in fifteen days' time, and I have found them ever beautiful, although often in contradiction to my most inner and most cherished sentiments. Have a little indulgence for my prose and grant fifteen minutes for its perusal.

Here is the text upon which your poem is supported. In choosing it as epigraph you have given enough to make understood the idea that you were about to embellish. Your work is very beautiful, although built upon a foundation utterly false. What might it have been if you had fitted it to a true foundation and had admitted it as such!

Now, the serpent was more subtil than any beast of the field, which the Lord God had made.   Gen. iii., 1.

This, if I am not mistaken, is taken from a translation of the *Bible*, made under the reign of King James, and printed by the express order of this monarch, to be read in the churches. Without considering any other translation, but examining only the English words of this text, they can be rendered thus in French:

"Or, le serpent était plus subtil qu'aucune bête du champ que le Seigneur Dieu eût faite."

According to the doctrine of Luther, which is yours and mine, you are a born interpreter of the Scripture in what concerns you; for I assuredly consider you of a sane understanding and of a just mind. But are you sure that this is the Scripture; and do you not fear to take as rule of your faith, what is not Scripture? Has Luther, in speaking of the Scripture, spoken of the Scripture of the Hellenists, of that of Saint Jerome, even of his own, or that of Calvin? Assuredly not, but of the original Scripture, of the Scripture of Moses; in a word, of that of the *Sepher*. Now do you know if the English translation that you quote renders the meaning exactly? If it renders it, I agree with you that all that you have said is just; that all the consequences that you have deduced are good; and that your poem is indeed an enormous mystery, the formidable meaning of which is made to terrify. But if your epigraph does not render a word of the original Hebrew text, if it has nothing of the thought of Moses contained therein, what does it all amount to? In partaking of a false notion, your sane understanding and your just mind tend only to lead you more and more astray; all your inductions are illusory, and your mystery is only a vain phantom that the breath of truth dissolves into smoke.

You are not the only one, my lord, whom the erroneous translations of the first chapters of the *Bœreshith* have led to baleful results. In the first centuries of Christianism, the men who were attracted by the *éclat* of its rites and the depths of its mysteries, were often savants, Platonic philosophers, who, tired of the corruption of polytheism, and the divagation of its mysteries, came into the bosom of the Divine Unity joined to the Word and to the Universal Soul, to disencumber themselves of that multitude of gods and goddesses, of demi-gods and heroes, the number of which had overwhelmed them. But often these men recovered from the first pleasing delight caused by the morals of the Gospel, its simple and consoling dogmas; profiting by a remnant of light in those dark days to fix the basis of the belief that was presented to them, they detached themselves brusquely from it with disdain. Such were Valentine, Basilius, Marcion, Apelles, Bardesanes and Manes, the most terrible adversaries that the *Bible* has encountered. All treated as impious the author of a book wherein the Being, good par excellence, is represented as the author of evil; wherein this Being creates without plan, prefers arbitrarily, repents, is angry, and punishes an innocent posterity for the crime of one whose downfall He had prepared. Manes said nothing else in his works than that which you have said in yours. Judging Moses according to the Greek book that is said to be his, this powerful heresiarch regarded the prophet of the Hebrews as having been inspired by the genius of evil.

And it was not only the men whom I have just named, or their sectarians, condemned as heretics, who felt these difficulties. Among the early fathers of the church, the wisest and even the most orthodox were struck by them. Saint Augustine agreed that there was no way of conserving the literal meaning of the first three chapters of Genesis without offending piety and without attributing to God things unworthy of Him. Origen declared that if one took the history of creation in the literal sense, it was absurd and contradictory. He pitied the ignorant ones who, led astray by the letter, and misunderstanding the spirit of the holy books, attributed to God sentiments and actions that one would not attribute to the most unjust and most barbarous of men. The wise Beausobre, in his *Histoire du Manichéisme*, and Père Petau, in his *Dogmes théologiques* quote a multitude of similar examples. The most striking is without doubt that of Saint Paul, who declares in innumerable passages that the letter killeth, and that the spirit maketh alive, and who, in his *II Epistle to the Corinthians*, gives clearly to be understood that Moses threw over his writings a veil which the vulgar of the Jews have not yet raised.

You see well, my lord, that the radical defect of the chapter from which you have drawn the text of your poem has been felt by others as well as by you. It was even to avoid the grave difficulties of consequences that might be drawn from it, that the Christian church enlightened by the storms excited by Marcion and Manes, took the prudent resolution of forbidding the people to read the holy books. The protestants cried out much against this interdiction, which they treated as tyrannical; but they did not see or did not wish to see that it was, in the condition of things, the best course to take; and that it was better to leave certain individuals ignorant in their ignorance than to give them, irrelevantly, a fatal knowledge that might bear them to their own destruction or to the destruction of others. This interdiction, limited, moreover, to the lower classes of society then plunged in darkness, was far from having the same disadvantages as the unlimited liberty allowed by Luther. This liberty, as you know, filled a crowd of stupid or fiery sectarians with sudden and silly presumption and persuaded them, in the midst of their stupidity or delirium, that they were sufficiently sane of understanding or sufficiently favoured of God to interpret the Scriptures. There sprung up in Germany and in England a swarm of opposed sects, of Moravians, Anabaptists, Puritans, Quakers, etc., who, from the beginning of the Reform, spread themselves afar and filled Europe with tribulations and murders.

It would have been better, undoubtedly, if the holy books had been translated in such a manner that they could have been put into the hands of all the world, leaving nothing for the arbitrary interpretation of anyone. But that could not be, since the Hebraic tongue being lost, a defective version had come into existence through the subtlety of the Essenes, and had usurped the place of the original text. Perhaps the Christian church might have recognized the evil sooner and found the remedy, by seeking to restore in all its splendour the sacred monument upon which it was founded; by that means it might certainly have avoided the disturbances caused by Wycliff and John Huss, and might not have been rent by the schism of Luther and of Calvin. It was only a question of finding a savant who would devote himself to reconstructing the fallen edifice of the tongue of Moses. This was difficult but not impossible, since it is seen that many men, of the Israelites, Mussulmans and Christians, have done it for their own use; and since finally I myself have done it, urged by the sole desire to know the origin of the universe, at a time when my plan was to write the history of the earth.

That I have succeeded in this enterprise appears to me beyond doubt, for the work that I have published upon this subject and circulated in somewhat large numbers, has been for some time in the hands of savants.[1] It was after having established this basis of the Hebraic tongue and while I was occupied with the Commentary that I had promised upon the *Cosmogony of Moses*, that your *Mystery of Cain* fell into my hands. I have told you, my lord, what effect I felt. Determined by a sudden impulse to interrupt my serious occupations, I entered into the poetical field, and I have translated your work in order to have the right to combat you. Permit me this, since from it there can proceed only glory for you. It is not a question here of poetry; yours is above all praise. It is only a question of consequences that you have made to follow certain cosmogonic acts, which an imperfect version (of which I have revealed the origin), has caused you to take for historic facts. Let us see what

---

[1] This work is composed of an Hebraic grammar founded upon entirely new principles; of a radical vocabulary; and a translation in English and in French of the first ten chapters of the *Bœreshith*, with copious notes, in which the meaning given to each word is proved by its radical analysis and is confronted with the corresponding words in the principal tongues of the Orient. *Hebraic Tongue Restored*, Fabre d'Olivet. Putnam, N. Y.

these acts are; let us read that which Moses wrote and not that which his translators have made him say.

What Moses wrote has already been published by me in the work that I have just cited. It would be too long to transcribe it in its entirety; and moreover, this transcription would engage me in explanations which would exceed the limits that I must place upon this letter. Let us content ourselves for the moment with some general ideas, to which I shall have occasion to return again. Let us take your epigraph alone, and see in what the copy differs here from the original.

The English translation that you have copied says, as we have seen: "Now, the serpent was more subtil than any beast of the field, which the Lord God had made."

And this is what Moses says:

והנחש היה ערום מכל חית השדה אשר עשה יהוה אלהים:

Wha-Nahàsh hatah hâroum mi-chol hàtath ha-shadeh asher hâshah Jhôah Ælohîm.

That is to say in English:

"Now Nahash (cupidity) was an insidious passion (blind principle) in all elementary life which Yahweh Ælohim had made."

You see, my lord, that there is therein, neither serpent, nor subtlety, nor beast, nor field. The Hellenist translators have said all these pretty things, either through ignorance, or as I myself suspect, through deliberate purpose. All the rest of the chapter is in keeping. After this example you can judge of the singular contrasts it presents. These translators, not wishing to tear away the veil that Moses had spread over the origin of evil, for fear of incurring the anathema hurled against all those who betrayed to strangers this terrible mystery, began here to thicken it with all their might. For them Nahash, cupidity, became *a serpent;* an insidious passion, a blind principle, became *a subtlety;* elementary life was transformed into *a beast;* and finally nature was nothing more than *a field.* What do you think of the travesty? Do you understand now the singular effect made upon me by your poem?

Whereas the lawgiver of the Hebrews, filled with a divine inspiration, rises to incommensurable heights; whereas he develops and makes the principles of the universe act in their universal origin; whereas he depicts their modifications and their particularizations, you, in the steps of his malicious translators, you see, in cosmogonic beings, men and women; and in the modification of these beings, historic facts, from which you draw consequences rigorously true for you, but nevertheless wholly fallacious.

Let us see first the characters that you give to your personages.

In your drama, Adam is a good man who allows himself to be governed by his wife, and who always does all that she wishes, believing that he follows only his own will.

Eve is a woman, passionate, clever, but violent and vindictive, sovereign over her husband whom she has subjugated, and to whom she feigns unceasingly to submit without ever fearing that he will dominate her.

Cain is a man of violent character, passionate but generous; capable of the highest virtues as of the greatest crimes according as he is moved; indomitable in his will, but susceptible to influence. He is remarkable for his great strength, which he uses for good as well as for evil.

His brother Abel has become, under your brush, a weak man, of gentle character, inclined to good, but without energy to manifest it.

Adah and Zillah are insignificant personages. There is in Adah, however, the rough outlines of a beautiful womanly character.

Let us now consider what these same personages are, not in the translators of Moses, but in Moses himself.

Adam, in his universal essence, cannot be explained without a previous instruction; for European civilization not being nearly so advanced as that of Asia and Africa was before Moses, it has not yet acquired the same universal thoughts, and lacks in consequence the terms to express them. These terms can only be formed as the thoughts are developed. One will find in the Commentary that I am preparing upon the cosmogony, all the data necessary to attain this purpose. Adam, in his particular essence, can be explained; although this idea, particularized in the thought of Moses, is still presented to us under an universal form. Adam is that which I have called the *kingdom of man*, that which has been improperly called *mankind;* it is *man*, conceived abstractly: that is to say, the general mass of all the men who compose, have composed or will compose *humanity;* who enjoy, have enjoyed or will enjoy *human life*. This mass, conceived thus as one sole being, lives a proper, universal life which is particularized and reflected in individuals of the two sexes. Considered under this latter relation, Adam is male and female.

Whether Adam is conceived in his universal or in his particular essence, Eve is always his creative faculty, his efficient force, his own will, by means of which he manifests himself exteriorly. In the principle of his universal existence, Eve is not distinguished from the universal creative faculty from which Adam emanates. It is not until the moment of his distinction that Adam becomes a free and independent being, and that he can exercise exteriorly, according to his own will, his efficient, creative force. It is always through Eve that Adam is modified in good or in evil. Eve makes for him everything within him and without him.

Cain and Abel are the two primordial forces of elementary nature. These are the first two cosmogonic beings produced by Eve, when after a certain movement toward elementary nature, she has lost her name of *Aïsha*, which designated the intellectual nature of Adam, to take that of Eve, which expresses no more than the material life of this universal being. It is in this material life that Cain and Abel took birth and that their principles, which were in power of being from the origin of things, passed into action to produce all that which must in the future constitute that life. Cain can be conceived as the action of compressive force, and Abel as that of expansive force. These two actions, issues of the same source, are hostile from the moment of their birth, according to the manner by which everything exists in nature. They act incessantly the one upon the other, and seek reciprocally to dominate, and to be reduced to their own nature. The compressive action, more energetic than the expansive action, always gains the ascendancy in the beginning; and overwhelming it, so to speak, compacts the universal substance upon which it acts, and gives existence to material forms that were not previously.

In personifying these two actions under the names of Cain and Abel, and in considering these two elementary beings as *brothers*, one has been able easily to see a *murder* in what was a cosmogonic act of momentary destruction, and poetically to call *fratricide* that destruction of the action of one by the other; so that thanks to the translation of the Hellenists, there has been transformed into an historical, positive fact, into a murder, into an execrable crime, into a fratricide at last, a cosmogonic act which began at the origin of elementary life, which still endures, and which will endure until this life gives place to another.

You see, my lord, that the beautiful verses you have made upon the pretended fratricide of Cain are completely wasted, at least as to the consequences that you have wished to infer for us. For the fatality of our destiny depends no more upon the fratricide of Cain than it does upon the fact that when fire has reduced bodies into vapours, these vapours, condensed by a certain elementary action, fall again as water, and extinguish the fire that gave birth to them. This cosmogonic act, which can be considered poetically as a permanent fratricide if the two elements of fire and water are considered as brothers, might be regarded as a parricide, if one were drawn along by some mystic allegory or by some bad interpretation of an ancient cosmogony to regard one of these two elements as the child of the other. This is precisely what has happened to several ancient nations, and particularly to the Greeks and Romans, who placed a parricide at the head of their cosmogony, in the same manner and for the same reasons that we have placed there a fratricide.

As Moses does not name the wives of Cain and Abel, whom you call Adah and Zillah, I shall say nothing except that if he had named them he would have considered them as plastic faculties of the cosmogonic beings to whom he gave them. Such is the consistent course that this hierographic writer follows in the explanation of his doctrine. I have explained in my book *La Langue Hébraïque Restituée*,[1] what should be understood by Adah and Zillah, wives of Lamech, and by Lamech himself. I shall return to these cosmogonic personages in the commentary that is to follow it.

As to Lucifer, the principal personage of your dramatic Mystery: this Lucifer, with a brilliant name that is due to a phrase badly interpreted from Isaiah, to whom you have given, my lord, a character so great, a style so grandiose, a power so vast—this Lucifer, I say, is not known to Moses as a distinct, independent being. The first hierographic writer who speaks to us on this subject is Job, who names him *Satan*, and who makes him appear in the presence of Yahweh with the other immortal spirits, called *Beni-Ælohim*, the sons of the gods. Moses also says of him that he is the production or rather the work of Yahweh, the Being of beings; but he gives him no other name than that of *Nahash*, which characterizes properly that deep, inner sentiment which attaches the being to his proper individual existence, and which makes him ardently desire to conserve it or to extend it. This name, which I have rendered by the word cupidity

[1] *Hebraic Tongue Restored*, Putnam, N. Y.

(original attraction), has been unfortunately translated in the version of the Hellenists as serpent; but never did it have this meaning even in the most vulgar language. The Hebrew has two or three words, entirely different from that one, to designate a serpent. *Nahash* is rather, if I can express it thus, that radical egoism which urges the being to make a centre of himself, and to draw everything to himself. Moses says that this sentiment is the blind passion of elementary animality, the secret spring or the leaven that God has given to nature. It is very remarkable that the name used here by the hierographic writer to designate this passion, this spring, this leaven, is *Harym*, the same that Zoroaster among the Persians used to designate the genius of evil. This name characterizes, in nearly all the idioms of the Orient, that which is central, hidden, mysterious, sealed, obscure. Thus according to the spirit of the *Sepher* and the true doctrine of Moses, *Nahash harym* would not be a distinct, independent being, such as you have depicted Lucifer, following the system that Manes borrowed from the Chaldeans and Persians; but indeed a central motive given to matter, a hidden spring, a leaven, acting in the profundity of things, which God has placed in corporeal nature to elaborate its elements.

We shall return again to this important subject in the course of the remarks that I propose making upon the most striking passages of your poem. It is enough for me to have first proved in this letter that the subject of the *Mystery of Cain*, in the manner in which you have presented it in your drama, is nowhere found in Moses; and that this subject, lacking foundation, is defective also in its forms, because all the characters therein are fantastic and deprived of truth. Therefore since the facts that you present as positive are illusory and are attached, not to human actions but to cosmogonic acts, the consequences that you have assumed by deduction are absolutely hypothetical, and are dissolved in thin air, even as I have already said.

So much for the physical part of the *Mystery of Cain*. As to the moral part, I shall give my opinion in brief reflections; and I hope, my lord, that you will be in no way offended to see me attacking principles that I believe subversive to society: principles that undoubtedly you have allowed to appear with regret, even at the very moment when you were forced by the inevitable consequences of your reasoning.

All of this, however, does not prevent your poem from conserving its poetical beauties. One only regrets that your admirable talent has not been exercised with a more profound understanding of the subject you wish to treat. What beautiful things you might have said! What sublime pictures you might have presented to the mind, if, instead of depicting Cain and Lucifer always in connivance, you had opposed the vain declamations of both to the magnificent expressions of a Being, possessor of the truth, who would have unfolded irresistible arguments! You were capable of doing it; I judge by the incredible force that you have used to make error triumph. It triumphs in your verses, that terrible enemy of truth; I have shuddered more than once in translating you. Nevertheless, however stirred, however appalled, I have never weakened your expression. Very far from your talent, without doubt, I have, notwithstanding, felt a certain pride in not keeping too much below my model;

as much to show to those who may read me with impartiality that the French tongue remains inferior in nothing to the English, as to testify to you while I combat you, the high esteem that I have for my adversary.

I should be extremely flattered, my lord, if you should judge thus of it, in receiving the assurance of the most distinguished sentiments with which I have the honour of being,

Your very humble servant,

Fabre d'Olivet.

Notice by Fabre d'Olivet

NOTICE BY FABRE D'OLIVET

THE letter written to Lord Byron discloses a part of the motives that determined me to translate his poem of *Cain;* but I have not entered with him into a discussion, which might appear to him uncalled for, upon the dangers that this work involves for the greater part of its readers. I was content to carry it into the fields of knowledge and of learning, and in speaking to him as one littérateur to another, to make him see, as was very well demonstrated for me, and very possible for him, that the bases upon which he raised his poetical edifice are illusory; that the events which he takes for historical facts are anything but such; and that, in consequence, all the inductions by which he triumphs in establishing the fatality of destiny and the dominance of the genius of evil on the earth, are false.

I do not know what effect the new knowledge that I have presented to him may have. I should wish, without doubt, that it might have adequate force to cause the light of truth to penetrate into a soul so lofty as his; and that he might be led by it to see the frightful dangers to which, in following a system so erroneous, he exposes not only himself, but also a great number of his fellowmen to whom he presents this destructive system invested with all the charms of a fascinating poetry. These dangers are assuredly very great; and I have felt them so much in reading his work, that, although

35

I was wholly absorbed at that time by labours of a captivating erudition, I have not hesitated an instant to tear myself from them and combat my adversary.

This adversary, following the footsteps of Epicurus, of Lucretius and of Bayle, renews, in other forms, the terrible arguments that these three men have in turn raised against divine Providence. Like them he strains to prove, although by different means, that this Providence does not exist; or that, if it does exist, its influence is null, since evil triumphs with impunity over the earth, delivering its inhabitants to the blind fatality of an irresistible destiny. According to the captious reasonings that he accumulates, and the fatal consequences that he draws from certain cosmogonic facts, he arrives at the same conclusions as Bayle, and leaves his readers in this cruel alternative, to wit: that God is weak, if He is good; wicked, if He is strong; or, if He is powerful and good, wholly alien to the destinies of man. He is weak if He is good, since wishing and owing the prevention of evil, He cannot prevent it; wicked if He is strong, because being able and owing the prevention of evil, He does not wish to prevent it; and finally, wholly alien to the destinies of man if He is powerful and good, since being able, constrained and wishing to render man happy, He leaves him, nevertheless, a prey to the most awesome calamities.

In a work that I published some years ago, *Les Vers Dorés de Pythagore*,[1] I exposed in all their force the arguments of Epicurus, of Lucretius and of Bayle, and I overthrew, by the dialectics of reasoning, the conclusions that these three philosophers had drawn by the same means; but

---

[1] *The Golden Verses of Pythagoras*, Fabre d'Olivet. Pub. Putnam, N. Y.

Lord Byron, although visibly imbued with the same maxims, does not follow the same paths. He does not reason as they do in a cold severe manner; he does not discuss the pro and the con with the calm of a rigorous logic. He flings himself audaciously into the midst of his subject and establishes himself as master there; and speaking with rare eloquence to the heart of man, awakens all its passions, arming their vehemence against him; he leads him by this road so much the more surely because he has used an unbounded art to hide from him the precipices with which it is bordered. The work in which he executes this design, premeditated or not (for the poets, it must be agreed with Plato, often strike goals that they have not seen), this work, I say, is so much the more dangerous since he draws its most redoubtable means from a sacred book, of which the reader accustomed to venerate the narrations, dares not invalidate the assertions, or even suspect that they might be invalidated. The author, quite at his ease on this point, having stated facts, the fatality and injustice of which he has no trouble in making felt, identifies his reader with the personages that he has put into the scene, and then leads him step by step, and from inference to inference, to draw for himself the conclusions of which I have spoken.

A theologian, or a man well versed in the controversy of the pulpit, would undoubtedly have no difficulty in seeing through the ruse of Lord Byron; and after having convicted him of error in faith, would easily prove to his readers the danger of his maxims, and would turn them away from the poet by warning them against the heretic. But I am not a theologian, and my position, **whatever Calvin** may have said, does not permit me to see heresy in another, since another might see it in me. I must not judge, according to the maxim of the Gospel, for fear of being judged; or see the mote in the eye of my brother while a beam is perhaps in my own.

Profoundly moved at the reading of the *Mystery of Cain*, I have not scorned it, as a sacerdotal man might have done, nor fought it as a doctor in theology might have done. I have approached it frankly as a littérateur, as a savant of the world; and the first thing that I have done is to sweep away from my antagonist the ground upon which he believed himself solidly supported. One certainly feels that the loss of this ground alone would take all his strength and reduce it to absurdity. But it might be possible for him to consider himself as unbeaten for all that, and despite all the proofs of reasoning and of fact contained in my letter, he might still claim his ground and pretend that it is by pusillanimity that I sought to oust him from it, not daring to fight him.

For this reason I shall renounce, in favour of the persons who could think as he does, all my advantages; and I shall consent to admit his ground under certain terms. I shall dare to attack him even there and shall prove to him, in the critical and philosophical remarks that I shall make upon his verses, that even in admitting the letter of the *Bible* and the most material meaning of the *Sepher*, without considering the spiritual and figurative meanings which are therein contained, his inductions are without foundation and are destroyed by the contradictions that they contain.

But perhaps it may be said that I have put too much

importance on a poetical work written in a foreign tongue, and that I could very well leave it without answer. As long as I had not read it, yes; but this was impossible from the moment that I had read it. The discourses of Cain and even those of Lucifer are only, in a lofty style, the same discourses that one hears held daily, in different styles, by men more or less polished, men who haunt the most brilliant salons of Paris and London, as well as the taverns and the most disgusting cabarets of these two capitals. Let me not be accused, however, of having made known these discourses, by translating them from English into French verse; for besides being already translated into prose (or about to be), they find, as I re-assert, their analogues in the mouth of more than one man frequenting the elegant cafés of the Palais-Royal or the obscure eating-houses of the Barrière du Maine.

If I have not taken the translation in prose which perhaps already exists, it is primarily because no prose renders the force of ordinary poetry, and still less that of English poetry. When one cannot understand this poetry in the original, it is impossible for any copy to retrace its idea. Our rhymed verses themselves are insufficient, as Abbé Delille has proved in his translation of Milton. A Frenchman who does not understand English perfectly must renounce ever knowing what English poetry of the kind of Lord Byron's is; or else he must admit verses of the same style, prosodic verses, such as those of which I gave example and of which I proposed admission in the introductory Dissertation that I placed in front of my examinations upon *Les Vers Dorés de Pythagore.*[1]

[1] *The Golden Verses of Pythagoras*, Putnam, N. Y.

I called them *eumolpiques* there, on account of the style of
the poetry to which I especially applied them, and which I
named *eumolpée* in opposition to *epopée*. But such verses,
which can be more generally called *prosodiques*, on account
of the prosody which is necessary, are likewise applicable to
all styles of poetry, as I have found since by experience.

It is, in a measure, to profit by the occasion which is
offered to use these verses in an important work that I have
composed them; also as I have intimated at the close of my
letter to Lord Byron, to uphold the French tongue against
the English tongue and to prove that it is inferior in nothing.
I certainly know that the reader, accustomed only to read
French prose or the rhymed verses of our tongue, will find
himself somewhat troubled; but may he have the kindness
to make this reflection: that of all the European tongues the
French is the only one which has not yet admitted this style
of poetry, and that it absolutely cannot go on without
remaining behind.

The difficulty that is experienced when one first reads
prosodic verses depends upon the practice one has with
rhyme. Consider this a moment: in this reading, all depends
upon the steady manner of scanning the lines, in observing
strictly the prosody, making the final masculine and feminine
felt, and enjambing one line boldly with another when it is
necessary, or when the meaning demands it.[1] The beauty
of this kind of verse depends upon the enjambment and
upon the manner of doing it. It is the same in Latin verse,

---

[1] I have already given, in the discourse upon the essence and form of
poetry that precedes *The Golden Verses of Pythagoras*, the rules for eumolpic or
prosodic verse. The principal of these rules consists in interlacing the finals
of different kinds; that is to say, of making a masculine line follow a feminine

in Greek verse, and generally in all unrhymed verse. Without enjambment, there can be only a wearisome and monotonous poetry. There is nothing more wretched than the rhythmic Greek or Latin verses if they do not enjamb. The English verses would be insupportable, by their lack of harmony, without the grace and force that enjambment gives them. Here lies all the difficulty, as much in the composition as in the reading.

If one wishes to give attention and if one observes the rules, few in number, that I have just given, I believe that in a very short time an educated Frenchman will read prosodic verse perfectly; and that not only will he be unaware that the rhyme is wanting, but he will even be vexed to find it incessantly. When it is presented to close a period, or to give more *éclat* to a description, it will give him an unlooked for effect and will cause him a pleasure that it did not cause him previously.

---

line, and a feminine follow a masculine, and never allowing a masculine or feminine line to contact a line of the same nature unless it rhymes. It is in this interlacing that the genius of the French tongue and the greatest force of its harmony reside.

Lord Byron's Preface

LORD BYRON'S PREFACE

THE following scenes are entitled "a Mystery," in conformity with the ancient title annexed to dramas upon similar subjects, which were styled "Mysteries, or Moralities" (1). The author has by no means taken the same liberties with his subject which were common formerly, as may be seen by any reader curious enough to refer to those very profane productions, whether in English, French, Italian, or Spanish. The author has endeavoured to preserve the language adapted to his characters; and where it is (and this is but rarely) taken from actual *Scripture*, he has made as little alteration, even of words, as the rhythm would permit. The reader will recollect that the book of Genesis does not state that Eve was tempted by a demon, but by "the Serpent"; and that only because he was "the most subtil of all the beasts of the field." Whatever interpretation the Rabbins and the Fathers may have put upon this, I must take the words as I find them, and reply with Bishop Watson upon similar occasions, when the Fathers were quoted to him, as Moderator in the Schools of Cambridge, "Behold the Book!"—holding up the Scripture (2). It is to be recollected that my present subject has nothing to do with the *New Testament*, to which no reference can be here made without anachronism. With the poems upon similar topics I have not been recently familiar. Since I was twenty, I have never read Milton; but I had read him so frequently before, that this may make little difference. Gesner's "Death of Abel" I have never read since I was eight years of age, at Aberdeen. The general impression of my recollection is delight; but of the contents I remember only that Cain's wife was called Mahala, and Abel's Thirza. In the following pages I have called them "Adah" and "Zillah," the earliest female names which occur in Genesis; they were those of Lamech's wives: those of Cain and Abel are not called by their names. Whether, then, a coincidence of subject may have caused the same in expression, I know nothing, and care as little.

The reader will please to bear in mind (what few choose to recollect) that there is no allusion to a future state in any of the books of Moses, nor indeed in the Old Testament (3). For a reason for this extraordinary omission he may consult Warburton's "Divine Legation"; whether satisfactory or not, no better has yet been assigned. I have therefore supposed it new to Cain, without, I hope, any perversion of Holy Writ.

With regard to the language of Lucifer, it was difficult for me to make him talk like a Clergyman upon the same subjects; but I have done what I could to restrain him within the bounds of spiritual politeness (4).

If he disclaims having tempted Eve in the shape of the Serpent, it is only because the book of Genesis has not the most distant allusion to anything of the kind, but merely to the Serpent in his serpentine capacity (5).

NOTE.—The reader will perceive that the author has partly adopted in this poem the notion of Cuvier, that the world had been destroyed several times before the creation of man. This speculation, derived from the different strata and the bones of enormous and unknown animals found in them, is not contrary to the Mosaic account, but rather confirms it; as no human bones have yet been discovered in those strata, although those of many known animals are found near the remains of the unknown. The assertion of Lucifer, that the pre-adamite world was also peopled by rational beings much more intelligent than man, and proportionably powerful to the mammoth, etc., is, of course, a poetical fiction to help him to make out his case (6).

I ought to add, that there is a "Tramelogedie" of Alfieri, called "Abel."—I have never read that nor any other of the posthumous works of the writer, except his Life.

Remarks Upon Lord Byron's Preface

REMARKS UPON LORD BYRON'S PREFACE

(1) The comparison that Lord Byron attempts to make between his poem of *Cain*, to which he gives the title of *Mystery*, and the early dramas which bore that title at the birth of the theatrical art in Spain, England, France or Italy, is wholly gratuitous. These early dramas, devoid of talent and of taste, are only remarkable for the extravagances, and often for the impieties that they contain. The magnificent talent that the English poet has displayed in his composition ought to have kept him from a comparison injurious to himself, whether it was made to bear upon extravagance or upon impiety. The *Mystery of Cain* is assuredly far from being extravagant, and I do not believe it is impious either, in the intention of its author. I think it is false in its principles, and illusory in its consequences, as I have begun to demonstrate in my letter to Lord Byron, and as I am about to continue to do in these remarks. This drama is entitled *Mystery* by imitation and not by comparison. It resembles the early Mysteries as the poem of Dante upon Hell, entitled *Comedy*, resembles the early comedies.

(2) In the emphasis with which the author quotes the text that he has chosen for epigraph, one feels all the importance that he puts into it. He thinks to triumph by its means, and reduce his reader to the necessity of receiving

the fatal consequences that he draws from it by the mouths of Cain and Lucifer. But, as I have proved to him in my letter, there is not one word of this text in Moses. It is in vain that he cries out with Bishop Watson, moderator in the schools of Cambridge: "Behold the Book!" This book that he shows me, and that he tells me is the Scripture, is simply the work of certain college pedants, paid by King James to translate into English the Hebrew that they did not understand any more than Bishop Watson understood it. It is true that there is in the aforesaid book, "now the serpent was more subtil than any beast of the field." But can one believe that Moses, that powerful theocrat, that sacred writer whom Longinius himself has quoted for his sublimity, in tracing with inspired hand the great Mystery of the universe, said such a thing? Supposing that he had wished to make an apologue, which certainly would not have been in place there, would he have chosen the serpent, that abject, repulsive animal, reduced to the most limited instinct, to represent the most cunning beast? The fox and the monkey, were they not there? See if Æsop is mistaken? When this fabulist puts the serpent in the scene, it is to make him commit an act of stupidity.[1]

Another point: Moses has said nothing in this passage of that which his English translators make him say, following the Essenes of Alexandria, who had their reasons for disguising the truth. I accuse these translators of ignorance, because none of these reasons could hold for them. Adhering to the doctrine of Luther, which declared that every man of a sane understanding and just mind was born interpreter

[1] In his fable of the Serpent and the File.

of the Scripture, they might have interpreted it worthily if they had understood it, without being held back either by the superstitious fears of the Essenes, or by the responsibilities of orthodox Christians. But these translators were ignorant ones, who, from the moment when they feigned to interpret the Hebrew and to render into English the meaning of the *Sepher*, interpreted only the Latin or the Greek; and instead of the original text, gave only an incorrect copy of the incorrect copy of the Hellenists of Alexandria.

Moses, I again repeat, does not speak in this famous passage either of serpent or of beast. He says that the original attraction, cupidity or radical egoism, was the impulsive passion, the secret, hidden spring of animal nature. I have proved the meaning that I give in this passage in my work *La Langue Hébraïque Restituée;* I have proved it in the strongest manner, by all the means that grammatical principles and philological learning can furnish. I shall prove it again in *La Théodoxie Universelle* which I am preparing, by all the moral and traditional inductions. But this is enough, perhaps too much, concerning this subject.

(3) It is certain that it appears thus when one consults only the version of the Hellenists, called the *version of the Seventy* or other vulgar translations calculated upon this one. The immortality of the soul is not proclaimed therein. But it is necessary to consider, to make this strange omission reasonable, that the knowledge of immortality was part of the mysteries. Therefore the Essenes, although they might admit the dogma, and although they might see it clearly contained in the text of the *Sepher*, could not, without betraying their oaths, allow it to appear in the version that

they were making for the profane. So they veiled it as much as they could; and here perhaps is one of the strongest proofs of the primal division of the sacred book into body and spirit. The karaite Jews and the Sadducees, who admitted only the letter, rejected the dogma of the immortality of the soul, which the Essenes and the Pharisees admitted, in receiving the spirit of the book and the oral tradition.

(4) Lucifer could not, indeed, express himself as a seminarist. The politeness of the spirits, or rather the spiritual politeness, that Lord Byron boasts of having given him, was not even essentially necessary. But still it is always pleasant to know what the politeness of Satan is; we shall remark upon it in its place. We shall also remark upon the passages where this personage sings the truth upon the lyre of Lord Byron, and where he makes heard a false or doubtful harmony.

(5) I have taken pains to make the author see that he is mistaken upon this decisive point. This point involves all the others, and gives in consequence a new physiognomy to the whole work.

(6) As it is not the question here of a geological system, we shall not dwell upon these details.

Cain

A Mystery

' Now the Serpent was more subtil than any beast of the field which the Lord God had made. "—Gen. iii., 1.

DRAMATIS PERSONÆ

MEN

Adam
Cain
Abel

SPIRITS

Angel of the Lord
Lucifer

WOMEN

Eve
Adah
Zillah

CAIN

ACT I

SCENE I

The Land without Paradise—Time, Sunrise
ADAM, EVE, CAIN, ABEL, ADAH, ZILLAH, *offering a
Sacrifice*

ADAM

GOD, the Eternal! Infinite! All-Wise!—
Who out of darkness on the deep didst make
Light on the waters with a word—all hail!
Jehovah, with returning light, all hail!

EVE

God! who didst name the day, and separate
Morning from night, till then divided never—
Who didst divide the wave from wave, and call
Part of thy work the firmament—all hail!

ABEL

God! who didst call the elements into
Earth—ocean—air—and fire, and with the day

And night, and worlds which these illuminate
Or shadow, madest beings to enjoy them,
And love both them and thee—all hail! all hail!

ADAH

God, the Eternal! Parent of all things!
Who didst create these best and beauteous beings,
To be beloved, more than all, save thee—
Let me love thee and them:—All hail! all hail!

ZILLAH

Oh, God! who loving, making, blessing all,
Yet didst permit the serpent to creep in,
And drive my father forth from Paradise,
Keep us from further evil:—Hail! all hail! (1)

ADAM

Son Cain, my first-born, wherefore art thou silent?

CAIN

Why should I speak?

ADAM

To pray.

CAIN

Have ye not pray'd?

ADAM

We have, most fervently.

CAIN

And loudly: I

Have heard you.

ADAM

So will God, I trust.

ABEL

Amen!

ADAM

But thou, my eldest-born, art silent still.

CAIN

'Tis better I should be so.

ADAM

Wherefore so?

CAIN

I have nought to ask.

ADAM

Nor aught to thank for?

CAIN

No.

ADAM

Dost thou not live?

CAIN

Must I not die? (2)

EVE

Alas!

The fruit of our forbidden tree begins
To fall.

ADAM

And we must gather it again.
Oh, God! why didst thou plant the tree of knowledge?

CAIN

And wherefore pluck'd ye not the tree of life?
Ye might have then defied him.

ADAM

Oh! my son,
Blaspheme not: these are serpents' words.

CAIN

Why not?
The snake spoke *truth:* it *was* the tree of knowledge;

It *was* the tree of life:—knowledge is good,
And life is good; and how can both be evil? (3)

EVE

My boy! thou speakest as I spoke in sin,
Before thy birth: let me not see renew'd
My misery in thine. I have repented.
Let me not see my offspring fall into
The snares beyond the walls of Paradise,
Which e'en in Paradise destroy'd his parents.
Content thee with what *is*. Had we been so,
Thou now hadst been contented.—Oh, my son!

ADAM

Our orisons completed, let us hence,
Each to his task of toil—not heavy, though
Needful: the earth is young, and yields us kindly
Her fruits with little labour.

EVE

                    Cain, my son,
Behold thy father cheerful and resign'd
And do as he doth.

                         [*Exit* ADAM *and* EVE

ZILLAH
Wilt thou not, my brother?

ABEL

Why wilt thou wear this gloom upon thy brow,
Which can avail thee nothing, save to rouse
The Eternal anger?

ADAH

My beloved Cain
Wilt thou frown even on me?

CAIN

No, Adah! no;
I fain would be alone a little while.
Abel, I'm sick at heart; but it will pass:
Precede me, brother—I will follow shortly.
And you, too, sisters, tarry not behind;
Your gentleness must not be harshly met:
I'll follow you anon.

ADAH

If not, I will
Return to seek you here.

ABEL

The peace of God
Be on your spirit, brother!
                    [*Exit* ABEL, ZILLAH, *and* ADAH.

CAIN (*solus.*)

And this is
Life!—Toil! and wherefore should I toil?—because
My father could not keep his place in Eden.
What had *I* done in this?—I was unborn,
I sought not to be born; nor love the state
To which that birth has brought me. Why did he
Yield to the serpent and the woman? or,

Yielding, why suffer? What was there in this?
The tree was planted, and why not for him?
If not, why place him near it, where it grew,
The fairest in the centre? They have but
One answer to all questions, "'twas *his* will,
And *he* is good." How know I that? Because
He is all-powerful must all-good, too, follow?
I judge but by the fruits—and they are bitter—
Which I must feed on for a fault not mine. (4)
Whom have we here?—A shape like to the angels,
Yet of a sterner and a sadder aspect
Of spiritual essence: why do I quake?
Why should I fear him more than other spirits,
Whom I see daily wave their fiery swords
Before the gates round which I linger oft,
In twilight's hour, to catch a glimpse of those
Gardens which are my just inheritance,
Ere the night closes o'er the inhibited walls
And the immortal trees which overtop
The cherubim-defended battlements?
If I shrink not from these, the fire-arm'd angels,
Why should I quail from him who now approaches?
Yet he seems mightier far than them, nor less
Beauteous, and yet not all as beautiful
As he hath been, and might be: sorrow seems
Half of his immortality. (5) And is it
So? and can aught grieve save humanity?
He cometh.

Enter LUCIFER

LUCIFER

Mortal!

CAIN

Spirit, who art thou?

LUCIFER

Master of spirits.

CAIN

And being so, canst thou
Leave them, and walk with dust?

LUCIFER

I know the thoughts
Of dust, and feel for it, and with you.

CAIN

How!
You know my thoughts?

LUCIFER

They are the thoughts of all
Worthy of thought;—'tis your immortal part
Which speaks within you. (6)

CAIN

What immortal part?
This has not been reveal'd: the tree of life
Was withheld from us by my father's folly,
While that of knowledge, by my mother's haste,
Was pluck'd too soon; and all the fruit is death! (7)

LUCIFER

They have deceived thee; thou shalt live.

CAIN

I live,

But live to die: and, living, see no thing
To make death hateful, save an innate clinging,
A loathsome and yet all invincible
Instinct of life, which I abhor, as I
Despise myself, yet cannot overcome—
And so I live. Would I had never lived!

LUCIFER

Thou livest, and must live for ever: think not
The earth, which is thine outward cov'ring, is
Existence—it will cease, and thou wilt be
No less than thou art now. (8)

CAIN

No *less!* and why
No more?

LUCIFER

It may be thou shalt be as we.

CAIN

And ye?

LUCIFER

Are everlasting.

CAIN

Are ye happy?

LUCIFER

We are mighty.

CAIN

Are ye happy?

LUCIFER

No: art thou?

CAIN

How should I be so?   Look on me!

LUCIFER

Poor clay!
And thou pretendest to be wretched!   Thou!

CAIN

I am:— and thou, with all thy might, what art thou?

LUCIFER

One who aspired to be what made thee, and
Would not have made thee what thou art. (9)

CAIN

Ah!
Thou look'st almost a god; and—

LUCIFER

I am none:
And having fail'd to be one, would be nought
Save what I am.   He conquer'd; let him reign!

CAIN

Who?

LUCIFER

Thy sire's Maker, and the earth's.

CAIN

                                 And heaven's,
And all that in them is. So I have heard
His seraphs sing; and so my father saith.

LUCIFER

They say—what they must sing and say, on pain
Of being that which I am—and thou art—
Of spirits and of men.

CAIN

            And what is that?

LUCIFER

Souls who dare use their immortality—
Souls who dare look the Omnipotent tyrant in
His everlasting face, and tell him, that
His evil is not good! If he has made,
As he saith—which I know not, nor believe—(10)
But, if he made us—he cannot unmake:
We are immortal!—nay, he'd *have* us so,
That he may torture:—let him! He is great—
But, in his greatness, is no happier than
We in our conflict! Goodness would not make
Evil; and what else hath he made? (11) But let him

Sit on his vast and solitary throne,
Creating worlds, to make eternity
Less burthensome to his immense existence
And unparticipated solitude!
Let him crowd orb on orb: he is alone
Indefinite, indissoluble tyrant!
Could he but crush himself, 'twere the best boon
He ever granted: but let him reign on,
And multiply himself in misery!
Spirits and men, at least we sympathise;
And, suffering in concert, make our pangs,
Innumerable, more endurable,
By the unbounded sympathy of all—
With all! But *He!* so wretched in his height,
So restless in his wretchedness, must still
Create, and re-create——(12)

CAIN

Thou speak'st to me of things which long have swum
In visions through my thought: (13) I never could
Reconcile what I saw with what I heard.
My father and my mother talk to me
Of serpents, and of fruits and trees: I see
The gates of what they call their Paradise
Guarded by fiery-sworded cherubim,
Which shut them out, and me: I feel the weight
Of daily toil, and constant thought: I look
Around a world where I seem nothing, with
Thoughts which arise within me, as if they
Could master all things:—but I thought alone

This misery was *mine*.—My father is
Tamed down; my mother has forgot the mind
Which made her thirst for knowledge at the risk
Of an eternal curse; my brother is
A watching shepherd boy, who offers up
The firstlings of the flock to him who bids
The earth yield nothing to us without sweat;
My sister Zillah sings an earlier hymn
Than the birds' matins; and my Adah, my
Own and beloved, she too understands not
The mind which overwhelms me: never till
Now met I aught to sympathise with me. (14)
'Tis well—I rather would consort with spirits.

LUCIFER

And hadst thou not been fit by thine own soul
For such companionship, I would not now
Have stood before thee as I am: (15) a serpent
Had been enough to charm ye, as before.

CAIN

Ah! didst *thou* tempt my mother?

LUCIFER

               I tempt none,
Save with the truth: (16) was not the tree, the tree
Of knowledge? and was not the tree of life
Still fruitful? Did *I* bid her pluck them not?
Did *I* plant things prohibited within
The reach of beings innocent, and curious

By their own innocence? I would have made ye
Gods; and even He who thrust ye forth, so thrust ye
Because "ye should not eat the fruits of life,
And become gods as we." Were those his words?

CAIN

They were, as I have heard from those who heard them,
In thunder.

LUCIFER

   Then who was the demon? He
Who would not let ye live, or he who would
Have made ye live for ever in the joy
And power of knowledge? (17)

CAIN

      Would they had snatch'd both
The fruits, or neither!

LUCIFER

     One is yours already,
The other may be still. (18)

CAIN

   How so?

LUCIFER

        By being
Yourselves, in your resistance. Nothing can
Quench the mind, if the mind will be itself
And centre of surrounding things—'tis made
To sway. (19)

CAIN

But didst thou tempt my parents?

LUCIFER

I?

Poor clay! what should I tempt them for, or how? (20)

CAIN

They say the serpent was a spirit.

LUCIFER

Who

Saith that? It is not written so on high:
The proud One will not so far falsify,
Though man's vast fears and little vanity
Would make him cast upon the spiritual nature
His own low failing. The snake was the snake—
No more; and yet not less than those he tempted,
In nature being earth also—*more* in *wisdom*,
Since he could overcome them, and foreknew
The knowledge fatal to their narrow joys.
Think'st thou I'd take the shape of things that die? (21)

CAIN

But the thing had a demon?

LUCIFER

He but woke one

In those he spake to with his forky tongue.
I tell thee that the serpent was no more

Than a mere serpent: ask the cherubim
Who guard the tempting tree. When thousand ages
Have roll'd o'er your dead ashes, and your seed's,
The seed of the then world may thus array
Their earliest fault in fable, and attribute
To me a shape I scorn, as I scorn all
That bows to him, who made things but to bend
Before his sullen, sole eternity;
But we, who see the truth, must speak it. Thy
Fond parents listen'd to a creeping thing,
And fell. For what should spirits tempt them? What
Was there to envy in the narrow bounds
Of Paradise, that spirits who pervade
Space—but I speak to thee of what thou know'st not,
With all thy tree of knowledge. (22)

CAIN

                   But thou canst not
Speak aught of knowledge which I would not know,
And do not thirst to know, and bear a mind
To know.

LUCIFER
And heart to look on?

CAIN

                 Be it proved.

LUCIFER
Dar'st thou to look on Death?

CAIN

                                He has not yet
Been seen.

LUCIFER

        But must be undergone.

CAIN

                                My father
Says he is something dreadful, (23) and my mother
Weeps when he's named; and Abel lifts his eyes
To heaven, and Zillah casts hers to the earth,
And sighs a prayer; and Adah looks on me,
And speaks not.

LUCIFER

        And thou?

CAIN

                        Thoughts unspeakable
Crowd in my breast to burning, when I hear
Of this almighty Death, who is, it seems,
Inevitable. Could I wrestle with him?
I wrestled with the lion, when a boy,
In play, till he ran roaring from my gripe.

LUCIFER

It has no shape; but will absorb all things
That bear the form of earth-born being.

CAIN

Ah!
I thought it was a being: who could do
Such evil things to beings save a being?

LUCIFER

Ask the Destroyer.

CAIN

Who?

LUCIFER

The Maker—call him
Which name thou wilt; he makes but to destroy. (24)

CAIN

I knew not that, yet thought it, since I heard
Of death: although I know not what it is,
Yet it seems horrible. I have look'd out
In the vast desolate night in search of him;
And when I saw gigantic shadows in
The umbrage of the walls of Eden, chequer'd
By the far-flashing of the cherubs' swords,
I watch'd for what I thought his coming; for
With fear rose longing in my heart to know
What 'twas which shook us all—but nothing came.
And then I turn'd my weary eyes from off
Our native and forbidden Paradise,
Up to the lights above us, in the azure,
Which are so beautiful: shall they, too, die?

LUCIFER

Perhaps—but long outlive both thine and thee.

CAIN

I'm glad of that; I would not have them die,
They are so lovely. What is death? I fear,
I feel, it is a dreadful thing; but what,
I cannot compass: 'tis denounced against us,
Both them who sinn'd and sinn'd not, as an ill—
What ill?

LUCIFER

To be resolved into the earth. (25)

CAIN

But shall I know it?

LUCIFER

As I know not death,
I cannot answer.

CAIN

Were I quiet earth,
That were no evil: would I ne'er had been
Aught else but dust!

LUCIFER

That is a grov'ling wish,
Less than thy father's, for he wish'd to know.

CAIN

But not to live, or whereof pluck'd he not
The life-tree?

LUCIFER

He was hinder'd.

CAIN

Deadly error!
Not to snatch first that fruit:—but ere he pluck'd
The knowledge, he was ignorant of death.
Alas! I scarcely now know what it is,
And yet I fear it—fear I know not what!

LUCIFER

And I, who know all things, fear nothing: (26) see
What is true knowledge.

CAIN

Wilt thou teach me all?

LUCIFER

Ay, upon one condition.

CAIN

Name it.

LUCIFER

That
Thou dost fall down and worship me—thy Lord.

CAIN

Thou art not the Lord my father worships.

LUCIFER

No.

CAIN

His equal?

LUCIFER

No;—I have nought in common with him!
Nor would: I would be aught above—beneath—
Aught save a sharer or a servant of
His power. I dwell apart; but I am great:—
Many there are who worship me, and more
Who shall—be thou amongst the first.

CAIN

                I never
As yet have bow'd unto my father's God,
Although my brother Abel oft implores
That I would join with him in sacrifice:—
Why should I bow to thee?

LUCIFER

                Hast thou ne'er bow'd
To him?

CAIN

    Have I not said it?—need I say it?
Could not thy mighty knowledge teach thee that? (27)

LUCIFER

He who bows not to him has bow'd to me!

CAIN

But I will bend to neither.

LUCIFER

           Ne'er the less,
Thou art my worshipper: not worshipping
Him makes thee mine the same.

CAIN

             And what is that?

LUCIFER

Thou'lt know here—and hereafter. (28)

CAIN

              Let me but
Be taught the mystery of my being.

LUCIFER

           Follow
Where I will lead thee.

CAIN

         But I must retire
To till the earth—for I had promised—

LUCIFER

           What?

CAIN

To cull some first fruits.

LUCIFER

     Why?

CAIN

To offer up
With Abel on an altar.

LUCIFER

Saidst thou not
Thou ne'er hadst bent to him who made thee?

CAIN

Yes—
But Abel's earnest prayer has wrought upon me;
The offering is more his than mine—and Adah—

LUCIFER

Why dost thou hesitate?

CAIN

She is my sister,
Born on the same day, of the same womb; (29) and
She wrung from me, with tears, this promise; and
Rather than see her weep, I would, methinks,
Bear all—and worship aught.

LUCIFER

Then follow me!

CAIN

I will.

Enter ADAH

ADAH

My brother, I have come for thee;
It is our hour of rest and joy—and we
Have less without thee. Thou hast labour'd not
This morn; but I have done thy task: the fruits
Are ripe, and glowing as the light which ripens:
Come away.

CAIN

See'st thou not?

ADAH

I see an angel;
We have seen many: will he share our hour
Of rest?—he is welcome.

CAIN

But he is not like
The angels we have seen.

ADAH

Are there, then, others?
But he is welcome, as they were: they deign'd
To be our guests—will he?

CAIN (*To Lucifer*)
Wilt thou?

LUCIFER

I ask
Thee to be mine.

CAIN

I must away with him.

ADAH

And leave us?

CAIN

  Ay.

ADAH

  And *me?*

CAIN

        Beloved Adah!

ADAH

Let me go with thee.

LUCIFER

No, she must not.

ADAH

          Who
Art thou that steppest between heart and heart?

CAIN

He is a god.

ADAH

How know'st thou?

CAIN

                    He speaks like

A god.

ADAH

So did the serpent, and it lied.

LUCIFER

Thou errest, Adah!—was not the tree that
Of knowledge?

ADAH

         Ay—to our eternal sorrow.

LUCIFER

And yet that grief is knowledge—so he lied not:
And if he did betray you, 'twas with truth;
And truth in its own essence cannot be
But good.

ADAH

         But all we know of it has gather'd
Evil on ill: expulsion from our home,
And dread, and toil, and sweat, and heaviness;
Remorse of that which was—and hope of that
Which cometh not.   Cain! walk not with this spirit.
Bear with what we have borne, and love me—I
Love thee.

LUCIFER

      More than thy mother and thy sire?

Adah

I do. Is that a sin, too?

Lucifer

No, not yet;
It one day will be in your children.

Adah

What!
Must not my daughter love her brother Enoch?

Lucifer

Not as thou lovest Cain.

Adah

Oh, my God!
Shall they not love and bring forth things that love
Out of their love? have they not drawn their milk
Out of this bosom? was not he, their father,
Born of the same sole womb, in the same hour
With me? did we not love each other? and
In multiplying our being multiply
Things which will love each other as we love
Them?—And as I love thee, my Cain! go not
Forth with this spirit; he is not of ours.

Lucifer

The sin I speak of is not of my making,
And cannot be a sin in you—whate'er
It seem in those who will replace ye in
Mortality.

ADAH

What is the sin which is not
Sin in itself? Can circumstances make sin
Or virtue?—if it doth, we are the slaves
Of——

LUCIFER

Higher things than ye are slaves: and higher
Than them or ye would be so, did they not
Prefer an independency of torture
To the smooth agonies of adulation
In hymns and harpings, and self-seeking prayers
To that which is omnipotent, because
It is omnipotent, and not from love,
But terror and self-hope.

ADAH

Omnipotence
Must be all goodness.

LUCIFER

Was it so in Eden?

ADAH

Fiend! tempt me not with beauty; thou art fairer
Than was the serpent, and as false.

LUCIFER

As true.
Ask Eve, your mother; bears she not the knowledge
Of good and evil?

ADAH

Oh, my mother! thou
Hast pluck'd a fruit more fatal to thine offspring
Than to thyself; thou at the least hast past
Thy youth in Paradise, in innocent
And happy intercourse with happy spirits;
But we, thy children, ignorant of Eden,
Are girt about by demons, who assume
The words of God, and tempt us with our own
Dissatisfied and curious thoughts—as thou
Wert work'd on by the snake, in thy most flush'd
And heedless, harmless wantonness of bliss.
I cannot answer this immortal thing
Which stands before me; I cannot abhor him;
I look upon him with a pleasing fear,
And yet I fly not from him: in his eye
There is a fastening attraction which
Fixes my fluttering eyes on his; my heart
Beats quick; he awes me, and yet draws me near,
Nearer, and nearer: Cain—Cain—save me from him!

CAIN

What dreads my Adah? This is no ill spirit.

ADAH

He is not God—nor God's: I have beheld
The cherubs and the seraphs; he looks not
Like them.

CAIN

But there are spirits loftier still—
The archangels.

LUCIFER

And still loftier than the archangels.

ADAH

Ay—but not blessed.

LUCIFER   .

If the blessedness
Consists in slavery—no.

ADAH

I have heard it said,
The seraphs *love most*—cherubim *know most*—
And this should be a cherub—since he loves not.

LUCIFER

And if the higher knowledge quenches love,
What must *he be* you cannot love when known?
Since the all-knowing cherubim love least,
The seraphs' love can be but ignorance:
That they are not compatible, the doom
Of thy fond parents, for their daring, proves.
Choose betwixt love and knowledge—since there is
No other choice: your sire hath chosen already;
His worship is but fear. (30)

Cain

ADAH

> Oh, Cain! choose love.

CAIN

For thee, my Adah, I choose not—it was
Born with me—but I love nought else.

ADAH

> Our parents?

CAIN

Did they love us when they snatch'd from the tree
That which hath driven us all from Paradise?

ADAH

We were not born then—and if we had been,
Should we not love them and our children, Cain?

CAIN

My little Enoch! and his lisping sister!
Could I but deem them happy, I would half
Forget—but it can never be forgotten
Through thrice a thousand generations! never
Shall men love the remembrance of the man
Who sow'd the seed of evil and mankind
In the same hour! They pluck'd the tree of science
And sin—and, not content with their own sorrow,
Begot *me—thee*—and all the few that are,
And all the unnumber'd and innumerable
Multitudes, millions, myriads, which may be,
To inherit agonies accumulated

By ages!—And *I* must be sire of such things!
Thy beauty and thy love—my love and joy,
The rapturous moment and the placid hour,
All we love in our children and each other,
But lead them and ourselves through many years
Of sin and pain—or few, but still of sorrow,
Intercheck'd with an instant of brief pleasure,
To Death—the unknown!　Methinks the tree of knowledge
Hath not fulfill'd its promise:—if they sinn'd,
At least they ought to have known all things that are
Of knowledge—and the mystery of death.
What do they know?—that they are miserable.
What need of snakes and fruits to teach us that? (31)

ADAH

I am not wretched, Cain, and if thou
Wert happy—

CAIN

　　　　Be thou happy then alone—
I will have nought to do with happiness,
Which humbles me and mine.

ADAH

　　　　　　Alone I could not,
Nor *would* be happy: but with those around us,
I think I could be so, despite of death,
Which, as I know it not, I dread not, though
It seems an awful shadow—if I may
Judge from what I have heard.

LUCIFER
And thou couldst not
Alone, thou say'st, be happy?

ADAH
Alone! Oh, my God!
Who could be happy and alone, or good?
To me my solitude seems sin; unless
When I think how soon I shall see my brother,
His brother, and our children, and our parents.

LUCIFER
Yet thy God is alone; and is he happy?
Lonely and good? (32)

ADAH
He is not so; he hath
The angels and the mortals to make happy,
And thus becomes so in diffusing joy:
What else can joy be but the spreading joy?

LUCIFER
Ask of your sire, the exile fresh from Eden;
Or of his first-born son; ask your own heart;
It is not tranquil.

ADAH
Alas! no; and you—
Are you of heaven?

LUCIFER
If I am not, inquire
The cause of this all-spreading happiness

(Which you proclaim) of the all-great and good
Maker of life and living things; (33) it is
His secret, and he keeps it. We must bear,
And some of us resist, and both in vain,
His seraphs say; but it is worth the trial, (34)
Since better may not be without: there is
A wisdom in the spirit, which directs
To right, (35) as in the dim blue air the eye
Of you, young mortals, lights at once upon
The star which watches, welcoming the morn.

ADAH

It is a beautiful star; I love it for
Its beauty.

LUCIFER

And why not adore?

ADAH

                Our father
Adores the Invisible only.

LUCIFER

              But the symbols
Of the Invisible are the loveliest
Of what is visible; and yon bright star
Is leader of the host of heaven.

ADAH

                Our father
Saith that he has beheld the God himself
Who made him and our mother.

LUCIFER

Hast *thou* seen him?

ADAH

Yes—in his works.

LUCIFER

But in his being?

ADAH

No—

Save in my father, who is God's own image;
Or in his angels, who are like to thee—
And brighter, yet less beautiful and powerful
In seeming: as the silent sunny noon,
All light they look upon us; but thou seem'st
Like an ethereal night, where long white clouds
Streak the deep purple and unnumber'd stars
Spangle the wonderful mysterious vault
With things that look as if they would be suns;
So beautiful, unnumber'd, and endearing,
Not dazzling, and yet drawing us to them,
They fill my eyes with tears, and so dost thou.
Thou seem'st unhappy; do not make us so,
And I will weep for thee. (36)

LUCIFER

Alas! those tears!
Couldst thou but know what oceans will be shed—

ADAH

By me?

LUCIFER

By all.

ADAH

What all?

LUCIFER

The million millions—
Thy myriad myriads—the all-peopled earth—
The unpeopled earth—and the o'er-peopled Hell,
Of which thy bosom is the germ.

ADAH

Oh Cain!
This spirit curseth us.

CAIN

Let him say on;
Him will I follow.

ADAH

Whither?

LUCIFER

To a place
Whence he shall come back to thee in an hour;
But in that hour see things of many days.

ADAH

How can that be?

LUCIFER

Did not your Maker make
Out of old worlds this new one in few days?

And cannot I, who aided in this work, (37)
Show in an hour what he hath made in many,
Or hath destroy'd in few?

CAIN

Lead on.

ADAH

Will he
In sooth return within an hour?

LUCIFER

He shall.
With us acts are exempt from time, and we
Can crowd eternity into an hour,
Or stretch an hour into eternity;
We breathe not by a mortal measurement—
But that's a mystery. Cain, come on with me.

ADAH

Will he return?

LUCIFER

Ay, woman! he alone
Of mortals from that place (the first and last
Who shall return, save ONE)—shall come back to thee
To make that silent and expectant world
As populous as this: at present there
Are few inhabitants.

ADAH

Where dwellest thou?

LUCIFER

Throughout all space. Where should I dwell? Where are
Thy God or Gods—there am I: all things are
Divided with me; life and death—and time—
Eternity—and heaven and earth—and that
Which is not heaven nor earth, but peopled with
Those who once peopled or shall people both—
These are my realms! So that I do divide
His, and possess a kingdom which is not
His. (38) If I were not that which I have said,
Could I stand here? His angels are within
Your vision.

ADAH

So they were when the fair serpent
Spoke with our mother first.

LUCIFER

Cain! thou hast heard.
If thou dost long for knowledge, I can satiate
That thirst; nor ask thee to partake of fruits
Which shall deprive thee of a single good
The conqueror has left thee. Follow me.

CAIN

Spirit, I have said it.

[*Exeunt* LUCIFER *and* CAIN.

ADAH (*follows, exclaiming*)
Cain! my brother! Cain!

ACT II

Scene I

The Abyss of Space

Cain

I tread on air, and sink not; yet I fear
To sink.

Lucifer

Have faith in me, and thou shalt be
Borne on the air, of which I am the prince.

Cain

Can I do so without impiety? (1)

Lucifer

Believe—and sink not! doubt—and perish! thus
Would run the edict of the other God,
Who names me demon to his angels; they
Echo the sound to miserable things,
Which knowing nought beyond their shallow senses,

Worship the word which strikes their ear, and deem
Evil or good what is proclaim'd to them
In their abasement. I will have none such:
Worship or worship not, thou shalt behold
The worlds beyond thy little world, nor be
Amerced, for doubts beyond thy little life,
With torture of *my* dooming. There will come
An hour, when toss'd upon some water-drops,
A man shall say to a man, "Believe in me,
And walk the waters"; and the man shall walk
The billows and be safe. *I* will not say
Believe in *me*, as a conditional creed
To save thee; but fly with me o'er the gulf
Of space an equal flight, and I will show
What thou dar'st not deny, the history
Of past, and present, and of future worlds.

CAIN

Oh, god or demon, or whate'er thou art,
Is yon our earth?

LUCIFER

Dost thou not recognize
The dust which form'd your father?

CAIN

Can it be?
Yon small blue circle, swinging in far ether,

With an inferior circlet near it still,
Which looks like that which lit our earthly night? (2)
Is this our Paradise? Where are its walls,
And they who guard them?

LUCIFER

                   Point me out the site
Of Paradise.

CAIN

             How should I? As we move
Like sunbeams onward, it grows small and smaller,
And as it waxes little, and then less,
Gathers a halo round it, like the light
Which shone the roundest of the stars, when I
Beheld them from the skirts of Paradise:
Methinks they both, as we recede from them,
Appear to join the innumerable stars
Which are around us; and, as we move on,
Increase their myriads.

LUCIFER

                 And if there should be
Worlds greater than thine own, inhabited
By greater things, and they themselves far more
In number than the dust of thy dull earth,
Though multiplied to animated atoms,
All living, and all doom'd to death, and wretched,
What wouldst thou think?

CAIN

　　　　　　　　　　　　I should be proud of thought
Which knew such things. (3)

LUCIFER

　　　　　　　　　　But if that high thought were
Link'd to a servile mass of matter, and,
Knowing such things, aspiring to such things,
And science still beyond them, were chain'd down
To the most gross and petty paltry wants,
All foul and fulsome, and the very best
Of thine enjoyments a sweet degradation,
A most enervating and filthy cheat
To lure thee on to the renewal of
Fresh souls and bodies, all foredoom'd to **be**
As frail, and few so happy—(4)

CAIN

　　　　　　　　　　　　Spirit! **I**
Know nought of death, save as a dreadful thing
Of which I have heard my parents speak, as of
A hideous heritage I owe to them
No less than life; a heritage not happy,
If I may judge till now. But, spirit! if
It be, as thou hast said (and I within
Feel the prophetic torture of its truth),
Here let me die: for to give birth to those
Who can but suffer many years, and die,
Methinks is merely propagating death,
And multiplying murder.

LUCIFER

Thou canst not
All die—there is what must survive.

CAIN

                                                The Other
Spake not of this unto my father, when
He shut him forth from Paradise, with death
Written upon his forehead.   But at least
Let what is mortal of me perish, (5) that
I may be in the rest as angels are.

LUCIFER

I am angelic: wouldst thou be as I am?

CAIN

I know not what thou art: I see thy power,
And see thou show'st me things beyond *my* power,
Beyond all power of my born faculties,
Although inferior still to my desires
And my conceptions.

LUCIFER

                                What are they, which dwell
So humbly in their pride, as to sojourn
With worms in clay?

CAIN

                                And what art thou, who dwellest
So haughtily in spirit, and canst range

Nature and immortality—and yet
Seem'st sorrowful?

LUCIFER

I seem that which I am; (6)
And therefore do I ask of thee, if thou
Wouldst be immortal?

CAIN

Thou has said, I must be
Immortal in despite of me. I knew not
This until lately—but since it must be,
Let me, or happy or unhappy, learn
To anticipate my immortality.

LUCIFER

Thou didst before I came upon thee.

CAIN

How?

LUCIFER

By suffering. (7)

CAIN

And must torture be immortal?

LUCIFER

We and thy sons will try. But now, behold!
Is it not glorious?

CAIN

Oh, thou beautiful
And unimaginable ether! and
Ye multiplying masses of increased
And still-increasing lights! what are ye? what
Is this blue wilderness of interminable
Air, where ye roll along, as I have seen
The leaves along the limpid streams of Eden?
Is your course measured for ye? Or do ye
Sweep on in your unbounded revelry
Through an aërial universe of endless
Expansion, at which my soul aches to think,
Intoxicated with eternity?
Oh God! Oh Gods! or whatsoe'er ye are!
How beautiful ye are! how beautiful
Your works, or accidents, or whatsoe'er
They may be! Let me die, as atoms die,
(If that they die) or know ye in your might
And knowledge! My thoughts are not in this hour
Unworthy what I see, though my dust is;
Spirit! let me expire, or see them nearer. (8)

LUCIFER

Art thou not nearer? look back to thine earth!

CAIN

Where is it? I see nothing save a mass
Of most innumerable lights.

LUCIFER

Look there!

CAIN

I cannot see it.

LUCIFER

Yet it sparkles still.

CAIN

What, yonder!

LUCIFER

Yea.

CAIN

And wilt thou tell me so?
Why, I have seen the fire-flies and fire-worms
Sprinkle the dusky groves and the green banks
In the dim twilight, brighter than yon world
Which bears them.

LUCIFER

Thou hast seen both worms and worlds,
Each bright and sparkling,—what dost think of them?

CAIN

That they are beautiful in their own sphere,
And that the night, which makes both beautiful
The little shining fire-fly in its flight,
And the immortal star in its great course,
Must both be guided. (9)

LUCIFER

But by whom or what?

CAIN

Show me.

LUCIFER

Dar'st thou behold?

CAIN

                              How know I what
I *dare* behold? as yet, thou hast shown nought
I dare not gaze on further.

LUCIFER

                    On, then, with me.
Wouldst thou behold things mortal or immortal?

CAIN

Why, what are things?

LUCIFER

Both partly: but what doth
Sit next thy heart?

CAIN

The things I see.

LUCIFER

                              But what
Sate nearest it?

CAIN

The things I have not seen,
Nor ever shall—the mysteries of death.

LUCIFER

What, if I show to thee things which have died,
As I have shown thee much which cannot die?

CAIN

Do so.

LUCIFER

Away, then! on our mighty wings.

CAIN

Oh! how we cleave the blue! The stars fade from us!
The earth! where is my earth? let me look on it,
For I was made of it.

LUCIFER

'Tis now beyond thee.
Less, in the universe, than thou in it:
Yet deem not that thou canst escape it; thou
Shalt soon return to earth, and all its dust;
'Tis part of thy eternity, and mine.

CAIN

Where dost thou lead me?

LUCIFER

To what was before thee!
The phantasm of the world; of which thy world
Is but the wreck.

CAIN

What! is it not then new?

LUCIFER

No more than life is; and that was ere thou
Or *I* were, or the things which seem to us
Greater than either: (10) many things will have
No end; and some, which would pretend to have
Had no beginning, have had one as mean
As thou; and mightier things have been extinct
To make way for much meaner than we can
Surmise; for *moments* only and the *space*
Have been and must be all *unchangeable.*
But changes make not death, except to clay;
But thou art clay—and canst but comprehend
That which was clay, and such thou shalt behold.

CAIN

Clay, spirit! What thou wilt, I can survey.

LUCIFER

Away, then!

CAIN

But the lights fade from me fast,
And some till now grew larger as we approach'd,
And wore the look of worlds.

LUCIFER

And such they are.

CAIN

And Edens in them?

LUCIFER

It may be.

CAIN

And men?

LUCIFER

Yea, or things higher.

CAIN

Ay? and serpents too?

LUCIFER

Wouldst thou have men without them? must no reptiles
Breathe, save the erect ones? (11)

CAIN

How the lights recede!
Where fly we?

LUCIFER

To the world of phantoms, which
Are beings past, and shadows still to come.

CAIN

But it grows dark, and dark—the stars are gone!

LUCIFER

And yet thou seest.

CAIN

'Tis a fearful light!
No sun, no moon, no lights innumerable.
The very blue of the empurpled night
Fades to a dreary twilight, yet I see
Huge dusky masses; but unlike the worlds
We were approaching, which, begirt with light,
Seem'd full of life even when their atmosphere
Of light gave way, and show'd them taking shapes
Unequal, of deep valleys and vast mountains;
And some emitting sparks, and some displaying
Enormous liquid plains, and some begirt
With luminous belts, and floating moons, which took
Like them the features of fair earth:—instead,
All here seems dark and dreadful.

LUCIFER

But distinct.
Thou seekest to behold death, and dead things?

CAIN

I seek it not; (12); but as I know there are
Such, and that my sire's sin makes him and me,
And all that we inherit, liable
To such, I would behold at once, what I
Must one day see perforce.

LUCIFER

Behold!

CAIN

'Tis darkness.

LUCIFER

And so it shall be ever; but we will
Unfold its gates!

CAIN

Enormous vapours roll
Apart—what's this?

LUCIFER

Enter!

CAIN

Can I return?

LUCIFER

Return! be sure: how else should death be peopled? (13)
Its present realm is thin to what it will be,
Through thee and thine.

CAIN

The clouds still open wide
And wider, and make widening circles round us.

LUCIFER

Advance!

CAIN

And thou!

LUCIFER

Fear not—without me thou
Couldst not have gone beyond thy world. On! on!
[*They disappear through the clouds.*

SCENE II

Hades

Enter LUCIFER *and* CAIN

CAIN

How silent and how vast are these dim worlds!
For they seem more than one, and yet more peopled
Than the huge brilliant luminous orbs which swung
So thickly in the upper air, that I
Had deem'd them rather the bright populace
Of some all unimaginable Heaven
Than things to be inhabited themselves,
But that on drawing near them I beheld
Their swelling into palpable immensity
Of matter, which seem'd made for life to dwell on,
Rather than life itself. But here, all is
So shadowy and so full of twilight, that
It speaks of a day past.

LUCIFER

It is the realm
Of death.—Wouldst have it present?

CAIN

                              Till I know
That which it really is, I cannot answer.
But if it be as I have heard my father
Deal out in his long homilies, 'tis a thing—
Oh God! I dare not think on't! Cursed be
He who invented life that leads to death!
Or the dull mass of life, that being life
Could not retain, but needs must forfeit it—
Even for the innocent! (14)

LUCIFER

            Dost thou curse thy father?

CAIN

Cursed he not me in giving me my birth?
Cursed he not me before my birth, in daring
To pluck the fruit forbidden?

LUCIFER

                  Thou say'st well:
The curse is mutual 'twixt thy sire and thee—
But for thy sons and brother?

CAIN

                  Let them share it
With me, their sire and brother! What else is
Bequeath'd to me? I leave them my inheritance.
Oh ye interminable gloomy realms
Of swimming shadows and enormous shapes,

Some fully shown, some indistinct, and all
Mighty and melancholy—what are ye?
Live ye, or have ye lived?

LUCIFER

Somewhat of both.

CAIN

Then what is death?

LUCIFER

What? Hath not he who made ye
Said 'tis another life?

CAIN

Till now he hath
Said nothing, save that all shall die. (15)

LUCIFER

Perhaps
He one day will unfold that further secret.

CAIN

Happy the day!

LUCIFER

Yes; happy! when unfolded
Through agonies unspeakable, and clogg'd
With agonies eternal, to innumerable
Yet unborn myriads of unconscious atoms,
All to be animated for this only! (16)

CAIN

What are these mighty phantoms which I see
Floating around me?—they wear not the form
Of the intelligences I have seen
Round our regretted and unenter'd Eden,
Nor wear the form of man as I have view'd it
In Adam's, and in Abel's, and in mine,
Nor in my sister-bride's, nor in my children's:
And yet they have an aspect, which, though not
Of men nor angels, looks like something, which,
If not the last, rose higher than the first,
Haughty, and high, and beautiful, and full
Of seeming strength, but of inexplicable
Shape; for I never saw such. They bear not
The wing of seraph, nor the face of man,
Nor form of mightiest brute, nor aught that is
Now breathing; mighty yet and beautiful
As the most beautiful and mighty which
Live, and yet so unlike them, that I scarce
Can call them living. (17)

LUCIFER
Yet they lived.

CAIN
                              Where?

LUCIFER
                                        Where
Thou livest.

When?

LUCIFER

On what thou callest earth
They did inhabit.

CAIN

Adam is the first.

LUCIFER

Of thine, I grant thee—but too mean to be
The last of these.

CAIN

And what are they?

LUCIFER

      That which
Thou shalt be.

CAIN

But what *were* they?

LUCIFER

       Living, high,
Intelligent, good, great, and glorious things,
As much superior unto all thy sire,
Adam, could e'er have been in Eden, as
The sixty-thousandth generation shall be,
In its dull damp degeneracy, to

Thee and thy son;—and how weak they are, judge
By thy own flesh.

CAIN

Ah me! and did *they* perish?

LUCIFER

Yes, from their earth, as thou wilt fade from thine.

CAIN

But was *mine* theirs?

LUCIFER

It was.

CAIN

But not as now.
It is too little and too lowly to
Sustain such creatures.

LUCIFER

True, it was more glorious.

CAIN

And wherefore did it fall?

LUCIFER

Ask him who fells.

CAIN

But how?

LUCIFER

By a most crushing and inexorable
Destruction and disorder of the elements,
Which struck a world to chaos, as a chaos
Subsiding has struck out a world: such things,
Though rare in time, are frequent in eternity.—(18)
Pass on, and gaze upon the past.

CAIN

'Tis awful!

LUCIFER

And true. Behold these phantoms! they were once
Material as thou art.

CAIN

And must I be
Like them?

LUCIFER

Let He who made thee answer that.
I show thee what thy predecessors are,
And what they *were* thou feelest, in degree
Inferior as thy petty feelings and
Thy pettier portion of the immortal part
Of high intelligence and earthly strength.
What ye in common have with what they had
Is life, and what ye *shall* have—death; the rest
Of your poor attributes is such as suits
Reptiles engender'd out of the subsiding
Slime of a mighty universe, crush'd into

A scarcely-yet shaped planet, peopled with
Things whose enjoyment was to be in blindness—
A Paradise of Ignorance, from which
Knowledge was barr'd as poison. (19) But behold
What these superior beings are or were;
Or, if it irk thee, turn thee back and till
The earth, thy task—I'll waft thee there in safety.

CAIN

No: I'll stay here.

LUCIFER

How long?

CAIN

For ever! Since
I must one day return here from the earth,
I rather would remain; I am sick of all
That dust has shown me—let me dwell in shadows.

LUCIFER

It cannot be: thou now beholdest as
A vision that which is reality. (20)
To make thyself fit for this dwelling, thou
Must pass through what the things thou see'st have pass'd—
The gates of death.

CAIN

By what gate have we enter'd
Even now?

LUCIFER

    By mine! But, plighted to return,
My spirit buoys thee up to breathe in regions
Where all is breathless save thyself. Gaze on;
But do not think to dwell here till thine hour
Is come.

CAIN

    And these, too; can they ne'er repass
To earth again?

LUCIFER

    Their earth is gone for ever—
So changed by its convulsion, they would not
Be conscious to a single present spot
Of its new scarcely harden'd surface—'twas—
Oh, what a beautiful world it *was!*

CAIN

    And is. (21)
It is not with the earth, though I must till it,
I feel at war, but that I may not profit
By what it bears of beautiful untoiling,
Nor gratify my thousand swelling thoughts
With knowledge, nor allay my thousand fears
Of death and life.

LUCIFER

    What thy world is, thou see'st,
But canst not comprehend the shadow of
That which it was.

CAIN

And these enormous creatures,
Phantoms inferior in intelligence
(At least so seeming) to the things we have pass'd,
Resembling somewhat the wild habitants
Of the deep woods of earth, the hugest which
Roar nightly in the forest, but ten-fold
In magnitude and terror; taller than
The cherub-guarded walls of Eden, with
Eyes flashing like the fiery swords which fence them,
And tusks projecting like the trees stripp'd of
Their bark and branches—what were they?

LUCIFER

That which
The Mammoth is in thy world;—but these lie
By myriads underneath its surface.

CAIN

But
None on it?

LUCIFER

No: for thy frail race to war
With them would render the curse on it useless—
'Twould be destroy'd so early. (22)

CAIN

But why *war*?

LUCIFER

You have forgotten the denunciation
Which drove your race from Eden—war with all things,
And death to all things, and disease to most things,
And pangs, and bitterness; these were the fruits
Of the forbidden tree.

CAIN

But animals—
Did they too eat of it, that they must die? (23)

LUCIFER

Your Maker told ye, *they* were made for you,
As you for him.—You would not have their doom
Superior to your own? Had Adam not
Fallen, all had stood.

CAIN

Alas! the hopeless wretches!
They too must share my sire's fate, like his sons;
Like them, too, without having shared the apple;
Like them, too, without the so dear-bought *knowledge!*
It was a lying tree—for we *know* nothing.
At least it *promised knowledge* at the *price*
Of death—but *knowledge* still: but what *knows* man?

LUCIFER

It may be death leads to the *highest* knowledge;
And being of all things the sole thing certain, (24)

At least leads to the *surest* science: therefore
The tree was true, though deadly.

CAIN

                             These dim realms!
I see them, but I know them not.

LUCIFER

                           Because
Thy hour is yet afar, and matter cannot
Comprehend spirit wholly—but 'tis something
To know there are such realms.

CAIN

                         We knew already
That there was death.

LUCIFER

        But not what was beyond it.

CAIN

Nor know I now.

LUCIFER

        Thou know'st that there is
A state, and many states beyond thine own—
And this thou knewest not this morn.

CAIN

                           But all
Seems dim and shadowy.

LUCIFER

          Be content; it will
Seem clearer to thine immortality. (25)

CAIN

And yon immeasurable liquid space
Of glorious azure which floats on beyond us,
Which looks like water, and which I should deem
The river which flows out of Paradise
Past my own dwelling, but that it is bankless
And boundless, and of an ethereal hue—
What is it?

LUCIFER

          There is still some such on earth,
Although inferior, and thy children shall
Dwell near it—'tis the phantasm of an ocean.

CAIN

'Tis like another world; a liquid sun—
And those inordinate creatures sporting o'er
Its shining surface?

LUCIFER

          Are its habitants,
The past leviathans.

CAIN

          And yon immense
Serpent, which rears his dripping mane and vasty
Head ten times higher than the haughtiest cedar

Forth from the abyss, looking as he could coil
Himself around the orbs we lately look'd on—
Is he not of the kind which bask'd beneath
The tree in Eden?

LUCIFER

Eve, thy mother, best
Can tell what shape of serpent tempted her. (26)

CAIN

This seems too terrible.   No doubt the other
Had more of beauty.

LUCIFER

Hast thou ne'er beheld him?

CAIN

Many of the same kind (at least so call'd),
But never that precisely which persuaded
The fatal fruit, nor even of the same aspect.

LUCIFER

Your father saw him not?

CAIN

No: 'twas my mother
Who tempted him—she tempted by the serpent.

LUCIFER

Good man! whene'er thy wife, or thy sons' wives
Tempt thee or them to aught that's new or strange,
Be sure thou see'st first who hath tempted *them*. (27)

CAIN

Thy precept comes too late: there is no more
For serpents to tempt woman to.

LUCIFER

But there
Are some things still which woman may tempt man to,
And man tempt woman:—let thy sons look to it!
My counsel is a kind one; for 'tis even
Given chiefly at my own expense: 'tis true,
'Twill not be follow'd, so there's little lost.

CAIN

I understand not this.

LUCIFER

The happier thou!—
Thy world and thou are still too young! Thou thinkest
Thyself most wicked and unhappy: is it
Not so?

CAIN

For crime, I know not; but for pain,
I have felt much.

LUCIFER

First-born of the first man!
Thy present state of sin—and thou art evil,
Of sorrow—and thou sufferest, are both Eden
In all its innocence compared to what
Thou shortly may'st be; and that state again,

In its redoubled wretchedness, a Paradise
To what thy sons' sons' sons, accumulating
In generations like to dust, (which they
In fact but add to,) shall endure and do.—
Now let us back to earth!

CAIN

           And wherefore didst thou
Lead me here only to inform me this? (28)

LUCIFER

Was not thy quest for knowledge?

CAIN

              Yes: as being
The road to happiness.

LUCIFER

          If truth be so,
Thou hast it.

CAIN

      Then my father's God did well
When he prohibited the fatal tree.

LUCIFER

But had done better in not planting it.
But ignorance of evil doth not save
From evil; it must still roll on the same,
A part of all things. (29)

CAIN

Not of all things. No:
I'll not believe it—for I thirst for good.

LUCIFER

And who and what doth not? *Who* covets evil
For its own bitter sake?—*None*—nothing! 'tis
The leaven of all life, and lifelessness.

CAIN

Within those glorious orbs which we beheld,
Distant and dazzling, and innumerable,
Ere we came down into this phantom realm,
Ill cannot come; they are too beautiful.

LUCIFER

Thou hast seen them from afar.

CAIN

                              And what of that?
Distance can but diminish glory—they
When nearer must be more ineffable.

LUCIFER

Approach the things of earth most beautiful,
And judge their beauty near.

CAIN

                              I have done this—
The loveliest thing I know is loveliest nearest.

LUCIFER

Then there must be delusion—What is that,
Which being nearest to thine eyes is still
More beautiful than beauteous things remote?

CAIN

My sister Adah.—All the stars of heaven,
The deep blue noon of night, lit by an orb
Which looks a spirit, or a spirit's world—
The hues of twilight—the sun's gorgeous coming—
His setting indescribable, which fills
My eyes with pleasant tears as I behold
Him sink, and feel my heart float softly with him
Along that western paradise of clouds—
The forest shade—the green bough—the bird's voice—
The vesper bird's, which seems to sing of love,
And mingles with the song of cherubim,
As the day closes over Eden's walls;—
All these are nothing, to my eyes and heart,
Like Adah's face: I turn from earth and heaven
To gaze on it.

LUCIFER

       'Tis frail as fair mortality,
In the first dawn and bloom of young creation
And earliest embraces of earth's parents,
Can make its offspring; still it is delusion. (30)

CAIN

You think so, being not her brother.

LUCIFER

Mortal!
My brotherhood's with those who have no children.

CAIN

Then thou canst have no fellowship with us.

LUCIFER

It may be that thine own shall be for me. (31)
But if thou dost possess a beautiful
Being beyond all beauty in thine eyes,
Why art thou wretched?

CAIN

Why do I exist?
Why art *thou* wretched? why are all things so?
Ev'n he who made us must be, as the maker
Of things unhappy! To produce destruction
Can surely never be the task of joy,
And yet my sire says he's omnipotent:
Then why is evil—he being good? I ask'd
This question of my father; and he said,
Because this evil only was the path
To good. (32) Strange good, that must arise from out
Its deadly opposite. I lately saw
A lamb stung by a reptile: the poor suckling
Lay foaming on the earth, beneath the vain
And piteous bleating of its restless dam;
My father pluck'd some herbs, and laid them to
The wound; and by degrees the helpless wretch

Resumed its careless life, and rose to drain
The mother's milk, who o'er it tremulous
Stood licking its reviving limbs with joy.
Behold, my son! said Adam, how from evil
Springs good!

LUCIFER

What didst thou answer?

CAIN

Nothing; for
He is my father: but I thought that 'twere
A better portion for the animal
Never to have been *stung at all*, than to
Purchase renewal of its little life
With agonies unutterable, though
Dispell'd by antidotes.

LUCIFER

But as thou saidst
Of all beloved things thou lovest her
Who shared thy mother's milk, and giveth hers
Unto thy children—

CAIN

Most assuredly:
What should I be without her?

LUCIFER

What am I?

CAIN

Dost thou love nothing?

LUCIFER

What does thy God love?

CAIN

All things, my father says; but I confess
I see it not in their allotment here.

LUCIFER

And, therefore, thou canst not see if *I* love
Or no, except some vast and general purpose,
To which particular things must melt like snows. (33)

CAIN

Snows! what are they?

LUCIFER

Be happier in not knowing
What thy remoter offspring must encounter;
But bask beneath the clime which knows no winter!

CAIN

But dost thou not love something like thyself?

LUCIFER

And dost thou love *thyself?*

Cain

                Yes, but love more
What makes my feelings more endurable,
And is more than myself, because I love it.

Lucifer

Thou lovest it, because 'tis beautiful
As was the apple in thy mother's eye;
And when it ceases to be so, thy love
Will cease, like any other appetite.

Cain

Cease to be beautiful! how can that be?

Lucifer

With time.

Cain

           But time has past, and hitherto
Even Adam and my mother both are fair:
Not fair like Adah and the seraphim—
But very fair.

Lucifer

              All that must pass away
In them and her.

Cain

              I'm sorry for it; but
Cannot conceive my love for her the less.
And when her beauty disappears, methinks

He who creates all beauty will lose more
Than me in seeing perish such a work.

LUCIFER

I pity thee who lovest what must perish.

CAIN

And I thee who lov'st nothing.

LUCIFER

And thy brother—
Sits he not near thy heart?

CAIN

Why should he not?

LUCIFER

Thy father loves him well—so does thy God.

CAIN

And so do I.

LUCIFER

'Tis well and meekly done.

CAIN

Meekly!

LUCIFER

He is the second born of flesh,
And is his mother's favourite.

CAIN

                     Let him keep
Her favour, since the serpent was the first
To win it.

LUCIFER

And his father's?

CAIN

                        What is that
To me? should I not love that which all love?

LUCIFER

And the Jehovah—the indulgent Lord,
And bounteous planter of barr'd Paradise—
He, too, looks smilingly on Abel.

CAIN

               I
Ne'er saw him, and I know not if he smiles.

LUCIFER

But you have seen his angels.

CAIN

            Rarely.

LUCIFER

                          But
Sufficiently to see they love your brother;
His sacrifices are acceptable.

CAIN

So be they! wherefore speak to me of this?

LUCIFER

Because thou hast thought of this ere now. (34)

CAIN

And if
I *have* thought, why recall a thought that—(*he pauses, as
agitated*)—Spirit!
Here we are in *thy* world; speak not of *mine.*
Thou hast shown me wonders; thou has shown me those
Mighty Pre-Adamites who walk'd the earth
Of which ours is the wreck; thou hast pointed out
Myriads of starry worlds, of which our own
Is the dim and remote companion, in
Infinity of life: thou hast shown me shadows
Of that existence with the dreaded name
Which my sire brought us—Death; thou hast shown me
    much—
But not all: show me where Jehovah dwells,
In his especial Paradise—or *thine:*
Where is it?

LUCIFER

Here, and o'er all space. (35)

CAIN

But ye
Have some allotted dwelling—as all things;
Clay has its earth, and other worlds their tenants;

All temporary breathing creatures their
Peculiar element; and things which have
Long ceased to breathe *our* breath, have theirs, thou say'st;
And the Jehovah and thyself have thine—
Ye do not dwell together?

LUCIFER

No, we reign
Together; but our dwellings are asunder.

CAIN

Would there were only one of ye! perchance
An unity of purpose might make union
In elements which seem now jarr'd in storms.
How came ye, being spirits, wise and infinite,
To separate? Are ye not as brethren in
Your essence, and your nature, and your glory? (36)

LUCIFER

Art thou not Abel's brother?

CAIN

We are brethren,
And so we shall remain; but were it not so,
Is spirit like to flesh? can it fall out?
Infinity with Immortality?
Jarring and turning space to misery—
For what?

LUCIFER

To reign. (37)

CAIN

Did ye not tell me that
Ye are both eternal?

LUCIFER

Yea!

CAIN

And what I have seen,
Yon blue immensity, is boundless?

LUCIFER

Ay.

CAIN

And cannot ye both *reign* then?—is there not
Enough?—why should ye differ?

LUCIFER

We *both* reign.

CAIN

But one of you makes evil.

LUCIFER

Which?

CAIN

Thou! for
If thou canst do man good, why dost thou not?

LUCIFER

And why not he who made? *I* made ye not;
Ye are *his* creatures, and not mine.

CAIN

             Then leave us
His creatures, as thou say'st we are, (38) or show me
Thy dwelling, or *his* dwelling.

LUCIFER

           I could show thee
Both; but the time will come thou shalt see one
Of them for evermore. (39)

CAIN

        And why not now?

LUCIFER

Thy human mind hath scarcely grasp to gather
The little I have shown thee into calm
And clear thought; and *thou* wouldst go on aspiring
To the great double Mysteries! the *two Principles!*
And gaze upon them on their secret thrones!
Dust! limit thy ambition; for to see
Either of these, would be for thee to perish!

CAIN

And let me perish, so I see them! (40)

LUCIFER
                    There
The son of her who snatch'd the apple spake!
But thou wouldst only perish, and not see them;
That sight is for the other state.

CAIN
                         Of death?

LUCIFER
That is the prelude.

CAIN
                    Then I dread it less,
Now that I know it leads to something definite.

LUCIFER
And now I will convey thee to thy world,
Where thou shalt multiply the race of Adam,
Eat, drink, toil, tremble, laugh, weep, sleep, and die. (41)

CAIN
And to what end have I beheld these things
Which thou hast shown me?

LUCIFER
                              Didst thou not require
Knowledge? And have I not, in what I show'd,
Taught thee to know thyself?

CAIN
                         Alas! I seem
Nothing.

Cain

LUCIFER

And this should be the human sum
Of knowledge, to know mortal nature's nothingness;
Bequeath that science to thy children, and
'Twill spare them many tortures.

CAIN

Haughty spirit!
Thou speak'st it proudly; but thyself, though proud,
Hast a superior.

LUCIFER

No! By heaven, which He
Holds, and the abyss, and the immensity
Of worlds and life, which I hold with him—No
I have a victor—true; but no superior.   (42)
Homage he has from all—but none from me:
I battle it against him, as I battled
In highest heaven. Through all eternity,
And the unfathomable gulfs of Hades,
And the interminable realms of space,
And the infinity of endless ages,
All, all, will I dispute! And world by world,
And star by star, and universe by universe
Shall tremble in the balance, till the great
Conflict shall cease, if ever it shall cease,
Which it ne'er shall, till he or I be quench'd!
And what can quench our immortality,
Or mutual and irrevocable hate?

He as a conqueror will call the conquer'd
Evil; but what will be the *good* he gives?
Were I the victor, *his* works would be deem'd
The only evil ones. And you, ye new
And scarce-born mortals, what have been his gifts
To you already in your little world?

CAIN

But few; and some of those but bitter.

LUCIFER

                                        Back
With me, then, to thine earth, and try the rest
Of his celestial boons to ye and yours.
Evil and good are things in their own essence,
And not made good or evil by the giver; (43)
But if he gives you good—so call him; if
Evil springs from *him*, do not name it *mine*,
Till ye know better its true fount; and judge
Not by words, though of spirits, but the fruits
Of your existence, such as it must be.
One good gift has the fatal apple given—
Your *reason:*—let it not be over-sway'd
By tyrannous threats to force you into faith
'Gainst all external sense and inward feeling:
Think and endure,—and form an inner world
In your own bosom—where the outward fails;
So shall you nearer be the spiritual
Nature, and war triumphant with your own.

                                        [*They disappear.*

ACT III

SCENE I

The Earth near Eden, as in Act I

Enter CAIN *and* ADAH

ADAH

Hush! tread softly, Cain.

CAIN

I will; but wherefore?

ADAH

Our little Enoch sleeps upon yon bed
Of leaves, beneath the cypress.

CAIN

Cypress! 'tis
A gloomy tree, which looks as if it mourn'd
O'er what it shadows; wherefore didst thou choose it
For our child's canopy?

ADAH

Because its branches
Shut out the sun like night, and therefore seem'd
Fitting to shadow slumber.

140

CAIN

Ay, the last—
And longest; but no matter—lead me to him.

[They go up to the child.

How lovely he appears! his little cheeks,
In their pure incarnation, vying with
The rose leaves strewn beneath them.

ADAH

And his lips, too,
How beautifully parted!   No; you shall not
Kiss him, at least not now: he will awake soon—
His hour of mid-day rest is nearly over;
But it were pity to disturb him till
'Tis closed.

CAIN

You have said well; I will contain
My heart till then.   He smiles, and sleeps!—Sleep on
And smile, thou little, young inheritor
Of a world scarce less young: sleep on, and smile!
Thine are the hours and days when both are cheering
And innocent! *thou* hast not pluck'd the fruit—
Thou know'st not thou art naked!   Must the time
Come thou shalt be amerced for sins unknown,
Which were not thine nor mine?   But now sleep on! (1)
His cheeks are reddening into deeper smiles,
And shinning lids are trembling o'er his long
Lashes, dark as the cypress which waves o'er them:
Half open, from beneath them the clear blue
Laughs out, although in slumber.   He must dream—

Of what? Of Paradise!—Ay! dream of it,
My disinherited boy! 'Tis but a dream;
For never more thyself, thy sons, nor fathers,
Shall walk in that forbidden place of joy! (2)

ADAH

Dear Cain! Nay, do not whisper o'er our son
Such melancholy yearnings o'er the past:
Why wilt thou always mourn for Paradise?
Can we not make another?

CAIN
Where?

ADAH
Here, or
Where'er thou wilt: where'er thou art, I feel not
The want of this so much regretted Eden.
Have I not thee, our boy, our sire, and brother,
And Zillah—our sweet sister, and our Eve,
To whom we owe so much besides our birth?

CAIN

Yes—death, too, is amongst the debts we owe her. (3)

ADAH

Cain! that proud spirit, who withdrew thee hence,
Hath sadden'd thine still deeper. I had hoped
The promised wonders which thou hast beheld,
Visions, thou say'st, of past and present worlds,
Would have composed thy mind into the calm

Of a contented knowledge; but I see
Thy guide hath done thee evil: still I thank him,
And can forgive him all, that he so soon
Hath given thee back to us.

CAIN

So soon?

ADAH

'Tis scarcely
Two hours since ye departed: two *long* hours
To *me*, but only *hours* upon the sun.

CAIN

And yet I have approach'd that sun, and seen
Worlds which he once shone on, and never more
Shall light; and worlds he never lit: methought
Years had roll'd o'er my absence.

ADAH

Hardly hours.

CAIN

The mind then hath capacity of time,
And measures it by that which it beholds,
Pleasing or painful; little or almighty.
I had beheld the immemorial works
Of endless beings; skirr'd extinguish'd worlds;
And, gazing on eternity, methought
I had borrow'd more by a few drops of ages
From its immensity; but now I feel
My littleness again. Well said the spirit,
That I was nothing!

ADAH

            Wherefore said he so?
Jehovah said not that.

CAIN

            No: *he* contents him
With making us the *nothing* which we are; (4)
And after flattering dust with glimpses of
Eden and Immortality, resolves
It back to dust again—for what?

ADAH

                 Thou know'st—
Even for our parents' error.

CAIN

            What is that
To us? they sinn'd, then *let them* die! (5)

ADAH

Thou hast not spoken well, nor is that thought
Thy own, but of the spirit who was with thee.
Would *I* could die for them, so *they* might live!

CAIN

Why, so say I—provided that one victim
Might satiate the insatiable of life,
And that our little rosy sleeper there
Might never taste of death nor human sorrow,
Nor hand it down to those who spring from him. (6)

ADAH

How know we that some such atonement one day
May not redeem our race?

CAIN

By sacrificing
The harmless for the guilty? what atonement
Were there? why, *we* are innocent: what have we
Done, that we must be victims for a deed
Before our birth, or need have victims to
Atone for this mysterious, nameless sin—
If it be such a sin to seek for knowledge? (7)

ADAH

Alas! thou sinnest now, my Cain; thy words
Sound impious in mine ears.

CAIN

Then leave me!

ADAH

Never,

Though thy God left thee.

CAIN

Say, what have we here?

ADAH

Two altars, which our brother Abel made
During thine absence, whereupon to offer
A sacrifice to God on thy return.

CAIN

And how knew *he*, that *I* would be so ready
With the burnt offerings, which he daily brings
With a meek brow, whose base humility
Shows more of fear than worship, as a bribe
To the Creator?

ADAH

Surely, 'tis well done.

CAIN

One altar may suffice; *I* have no offering.

ADAH

The fruits of the earth, the early, beautiful
Blossom and bud, and bloom of flowers, and fruits;
These are a goodly offering to the Lord,
Given with a gentle and a contrite spirit.

CAIN

I have toil'd, and till'd, and sweaten in the sun
According to the curse:—must I do more?
For what should I be gentle? for a war
With all the elements ere they will yield
The bread we eat? For what must I be grateful?
For being dust, and groveling in the dust,
Till I return to dust? (8) If I am nothing—
For nothing shall I be an hypocrite,
And seem well-pleased with pain? For what should I
Be contrite? for my father's sin, already

Expiate with what we all have undergone,
And to be more than expiated by
The ages prophesied, upon our seed.
Little deems our young blooming sleeper, there,
The germs of an eternal misery
To myriads are within him! better 'twere
I snatch'd him in his sleep, and dash'd him 'gainst
The rocks, than let him live to——

ADAH

Oh, my God!
Touch not the child—my child! *thy* child! Oh Cain!

CAIN

Fear not! for all the stars, and all the power
Which sways them, I would not accost yon infant
With ruder greeting than a father's kiss.

ADAH

Then, why so awful in thy speech?

CAIN

I said,
'Twere better that he ceased to live, than give
Life to so much of sorrow as he must
Endure, and, harder still, bequeath; but since
That saying jars you, let us only say—
'Twere better that he never had been born.

ADAH

Oh, do not say so! Where were then the joys,
The mother's joys of watching, nourishing,

And loving him? Soft! he awakes. Sweet Enoch!

[*She goes to the child.*]

Oh Cain! look on him; see how full of life,
Of strength, of bloom, of beauty, and of joy,
How like to me—how like to thee, when gentle,
For *then* we are *all* alike; is't not so, Cain?
Mother, and sire, and son, our features are
Reflected in each other; as they are
In the clear waters, when *they* are *gentle*, and
When *thou* art *gentle*. Love us, then, my Cain!
And love thyself for our sakes, for we love thee.
Look! how he laughs and stretches out his arms,
And opens wide his blue eyes upon thine,
To hail his father; while his little form
Flutters as wing'd with joy. Talk not of pain!
The childless cherubs well might envy thee
The pleasures of a parent! Bless him, Cain!
As yet he hath no words to thank thee, but
His heart will, and thine own too.

CAIN

Bless thee, boy!
If that a mortal blessing may avail thee,
To save thee from the serpent's curse!

ADAH

It shall.
Surely a father's blessing may avert
A reptile's subtlety.

CAIN

Of that I doubt;
But bless him ne'er the less.

ADAH

Our brother comes.

CAIN

Thy brother Abel.

Enter ABEI

ABEI

Welcome, Cain! My brother,
The peace of God be on thee!

CAIN

Abel, hail!

ABEL

Our sister tells me that thou hast been wandering,
In high communion with a spirit, far
Beyond our wonted range. Was he of those
We have seen and spoken with, like to our father?

CAIN

No.

ABEL

Why then commune with him? he may be
A foe to the Most High.

CAIN

And friend to man.
Has the Most High been so—if so you term him?

ABEL

Term him! your words are strange to-day, my brother.
My sister Adah, leave us for a while—
We mean to sacrifice.

ADAH

Farewell, my Cain;
But first embrace thy son. May his soft spirit,
And Abel's pious ministry, recall thee
To peace and holiness!

[*Exit* ADAH, *with her child.*

ABEL

Where hast thou been?

CAIN

I know not.

ABEL

Nor what thou hast seen?

CAIN

The dead,
The immortal, the unbounded, the omnipotent,
The overpowering mysteries of space—
The innumerable worlds that were and are—
A whirlwind of such overwhelming things,
Suns, moons, and earths, upon their loud-voiced spheres

Singing in thunder round me, as have made me
Unfit for mortal converse: leave me, Abel.

ABEL

Thine eyes are flashing with unnatural light—
Thy cheek is flush'd with an unnatural hue—
Thy words are fraught with an unnatural sound—
What may this mean? (9)

CAIN

It means—I pray thee, leave me.

ABEL

Not till we have pray'd and sacrificed together.

CAIN

Abel, I pray thee, sacrifice alone—
Jehovah loves thee well.

ABEL

Both well, I hope.

CAIN

But thee the better: I care not for that;
Thou art fitter for his worship than I am:
Revere him, then—but let it be alone—
At least, without me.

ABEL

Brother, I should ill
Deserve the name of our great father's son,

If as my elder I revered thee not,
And in the worship of our God call'd not
On thee to join me, and precede me in
Our priesthood—'tis thy place.

CAIN
                            But I have ne'er
Asserted it.

ABEL
                The more my grief; I pray thee
To do so now: thy soul seems labouring in
Some strong delusion; it will calm thee.

CAIN
                                    No;
Nothing can calm me more. *Calm!* say I? Never
Knew I what calm was in the soul, although
I have seen the elements still'd. My Abel, leave me!
Or let me leave thee to thy pious purpose.

ABEL
Neither; we must perform our task together.
Spurn me not. (10)

CAIN
            If it must be so—well, then,
What shall I do?

ABEL
            Choose one of those two altars.

CAIN

Choose for me: they to me are so much turf
And stone.

ABEL

Choose thou!

CAIN

I have chosen.

ABEL

'Tis the highest,
And suits thee, as the elder. Now prepare
Thine offerings.

CAIN

Where are thine?

ABEL

Behold them here—
The firstlings of the flock, and fat thereof—
A shepherd's humble offering.

CAIN

I have no flocks;
I am a tiller of the ground, and must
Yield what it yieldeth to my toil—its fruit:

[*He gathers fruits.*

Behold them in their various bloom and ripeness.

[*They dress their altars, and kindle a flame upon them.*

ABEL

My brother, as the elder, offer first
Thy prayer and thanksgiving with sacrifice.

CAIN

No—I am new to this; lead thou the way,
And I will follow—as I may.

ABEL (*kneeling*)

Oh God!

Who made us, and who breathed the breath of life
Within our nostrils, who hath blessed us,
And spared, despite our father's sin, to make
His children all lost, as they might have been,
Had not thy justice been so temper'd with
The mercy which is thy delight, as to
Accord a pardon like a Paradise,
Compared with our great crimes:—Sole Lord of light!
Of good, and glory, and eternity;
Without whom all were evil, and with whom
Nothing can err, except to some good end
Of thine omnipotent benevolence—
Inscrutable, but still to be fulfill'd—
Accept from out thy humble first of shepherd's
First of the first-born flocks—an offering,
In itself nothing—as what offering can be
Aught unto thee?—but yet accept it for
The thanksgiving of him who spreads it in
The face of thy high heaven, bowing his own
Even to the dust, of which he is, in honour

Of thee, and of thy name, for evermore! (11)
CAIN (*standing erect during this speech*)
Spirit! whate'er or whosoe'er thou art,
Omnipotent, it may be—and, if good,
Shown in the exemption of thy deeds from evil;
Jehovah upon earth! and God in heaven!
And it may be with other names, because
Thine attributes seem many, as thy works:—
If thou must be propitiated with prayers,
Take them! If thou must be induced with altars,
And soften'd with a sacrifice, receive them!
Two beings here erect them unto thee.
If thou lov'st blood, the shepherd's shrine, which smokes
On my right hand, hath shed it for thy service
In the first of his flock, whose limbs now reek
In sanguinary incense to thy skies;
Or if the sweet and blooming fruits of earth,
And milder seasons, which the unstain'd turf
I spread them on now offers in the face
Of the broad sun which ripen'd them, may seem
Good to thee, inasmuch as they have not
Suffer'd in limb or life, and rather form
A sample of thy works, than supplication
To look on ours! If a shrine without victim,
And altar without gore, may win thy favour,
Look on it! and for him who dresseth it,
He is—such as thou mad'st him;—and seeks nothing
Which must be won by kneeling: if he's evil,
Strike him! thou art omnipotent, and may'st,—
For what can he oppose? If he be good,

Strike him, or spare him, as thou wilt! since all
Rests upon thee; and good and evil seem
To have no power themselves, save in thy will;
And whether that be good or ill I know not,
Not being omnipotent, nor fit to judge
Omnipotence, but merely to endure
Its mandate; which thus far I have endured. (12)

The fire upon the altar of ABEL *kindles into a column of the
brightest flame, and ascends to heaven; while a whirlwind
throws down the altar of* CAIN, *and scatters the fruits
abroad upon the earth.*

ABEL (*kneeling*)

Oh, brother, pray! Jehovah's wroth with thee!

CAIN

Why so?

ABEL

Thy fruits are scatter'd on the earth. (13)

CAIN

From earth they came, to earth let them return;
Their seed will bear fresh fruit there ere the summer:
Thy burnt flesh-off'ring prospers better; see
How heav'n licks up the flames, when thick with blood!

ABEL

Think not upon my off'ring's acceptance,
But make another of thine own before
It is too late.

CAIN

I will build no more altars,
Nor suffer any.—

ABEL (*rising*)

Cain! what meanest thou?

CAIN

To cast down yon vile flatt'rer of the clouds,
The smoky harbinger of thy dull pray'rs—
Thine altar, with its blood of lambs and kids,
Which fed on milk, to be destroy'd in blood.

ABEL (*opposing him*)

Thou shalt not:—add not impious works to impious
Words! let that altar stand—'tis hallow'd now
By the immortal pleasure of Jehovah,
In his acceptance of the victims.

CAIN

His!

His pleasure! what was his high pleasure in
The fumes of scorching flesh and smoking blood,
To the pain of the bleating mothers, which
Still yearn for their dead offspring? or the pangs
Of the sad ignorant victims underneath
Thy pious knife? Give way! this bloody record
Shall not stand in the sun, to shame creation!

ABEL

Brother, give back! thou shalt not touch my altar
With violence: if that thou wilt adopt it,
To try another sacrifice, 'tis thine.

CAIN

Another sacrifice! Give way, or else
That sacrifice may be—

ABEL

What meanest thou?

CAIN

Give—

Give way!—thy God loves blood!—then look to it:—
Give way, ere he hath *more!*

ABEL

In *his* great name,
I stand between thee and the shrine which hath
Had his acceptance.

CAIN

If thou lov'st thyself,
Stand back till I have strew'd this turf along
Its native soil:—else—

ABEL (*opposing him*)

I love God far more
Than life.

CAIN (*striking him with a brand, on the temples, which he snatches from the altar*)

Then take thy life unto thy God,
Since he loves lives.

ABEL (*falls*)

What hast thou done, my brother? (14)

CAIN

Brother!

ABEL

Oh, God! receive thy servant, and
Forgive his slayer, for he knew not what
He did.—Cain, give me—give me thy hand; and tell
Poor Zillah——

CAIN (*after a moment's stupefaction*)

My hand! 'tis all red, and with—
What?

[*A long pause.—Looking slowly round.*

Where am I? alone! Where's Abel? where
Cain? Can it be that I am he? My brother,
Awake!—why liest thou so on the green earth?
'Tis not the hour of slumber:—why so pale?
What, hast thou!—thou wert full of life this morn!
Abel! I pray thee, mock me not! I smote
Too fiercely, but not fatally. Ah, why
Would'st thou oppose me? This is mockery;
And only done to daunt me:—'twas a blow—
And but a blow. Stir—stir—nay, only stir!

Why, so—that's well! thou breath'st! breathe upon me!
Oh, God! Oh, God!

ABEL (*very faintly*)

What's he who speaks of God?

CAIN

Thy murderer. (15)

ABEL

Then may God forgive him! Cain,
Comfort poor Zillah:—she has but one brother
Now.

[ABEL *dies.*

CAIN

And I none!—Who makes me brotherless?
His eyes are open! then he is not dead!
Death is like sleep; and sleep shuts down our lids.
His lips, too, are apart; why then he breathes!
And yet I feel it not.—His heart!—his heart!—
Let me see, doth it beat?—methinks—No!—no!
This is a vision, else I am become
The native of another and worse world.
The earth swims round me:—what is this?—'tis wet;
[*Puts his hand to his brow, and then looks at it.*
And yet there are no dews! 'Tis blood—my blood—
My brother's and my own; and shed by me!
Then what have I further to do with life,
Since I have taken life from my own flesh?
But he can not be dead!—Is silence death?

No; he will wake: then let me watch by him.
Life cannot be so slight, as to be quench'd
Thus quickly!—he hath spoken to me since—
What shall I say to him?—My brother!—No;
He will not answer to that name; for brethren
Smite not each other. Yet—yet—speak to me.
Oh! for a word more of that gentle voice,
That I may bear to hear my own again!

Enter Zillah

Zillah

I heard a heavy sound: what can it be?
'Tis Cain; and watching by my husband. What
Dost thou there, brother? Doth he sleep? Oh! heav'n!
What means this paleness, and yon stream?—No! no!
It is not blood; for who would shed his blood?
Abel! what's this?—who hath done this? He moves not;
He breathes not: and his hands drop down from mine
With stony lifelessness! Ah! cruel Cain!
Why cam'st thou not in time to save him from
This violence? Whatever hath assail'd him,
Thou wert the stronger, and should'st have stepp'd in
Between him and aggression! Father!—Eve!—
Adah!—come hither! Death is in the world! (16)
　　　　　[*Exit* Zillah, *calling on her parents, &c.*

Cain (*solus*)

And who hath brought him there?—I—who abhor
The name of Death so deeply, that the thought

Empoison'd all my life, before I knew
His aspect—I have led him here, and giv'n
My brother to his cold and still embrace,
As if he would not have asserted his
Inexorable claim without my aid.
I am awake at last—a dreary dream
Had madden'd me;—but *he* shall ne'er awake!

Enter ADAM, EVE, ADAH, *and* ZILLAH

ADAM

A voice of wo from Zillah brings me here.—
What do I see?—'Tis true!—My son!—my son!
Woman, behold the serpent's work, and thine!

[*To* EVE.

EVE

Oh! speak not of it now: the serpent's fangs
Are in my heart. (17)　My best beloved, Abel!
Jehovah! this is punishment beyond
A mother's sin, to take *him* from me!

ADAM

Who,
Or what hath done this deed?—speak, Cain, since thou
Wert present; was it some more hostile angel,
Who walks not with Jehovah? or some wild
Brute of the forest?

EVE

Ah! a livid light
Breaks through, as from a thunder-cloud! yon brand,

Massy and bloody! snatch'd from off the altar,
And black with smoke, and red with—

ADAM
                       Speak, my son!
Speak, and assure us, wretched as we are,
That we are not more miserable still.

ADAH

Speak, Cain! and say it was not *thou!*

EVE
                  It was.
I see it now—he hangs his guilty head.
And covers his ferocious eye with hands
Incarnadine.

ADAH
        Mother, thou dost him wrong—
Cain! clear thee from this horrible accusal,
Which grief wrings from our parent.

EVE
             Hear, Jehovah!
May the eternal serpent's curse be on him!
For he was fitter for his seed than ours.
May all his days be desolate! May—

ADAH
             Hold!
Curse him not, mother, for he is thy son—

Curse him not, mother, for he is my brother,
And my betroth'd.

EVE

            He hath left thee no brother—
Zillah no husband—me *no son!*—for thus
I curse him from my sight for evermore!
All bonds I break between us, as he broke
That of his nature, in yon—Oh death! death!
Why didst thou not take *me*, who first incurr'd thee?
Why dost thou not so now?

ADAM

            Eve! let not this,
Thy natural grief, lead to impiety!
A heavy doom was long forespoken to us;
And now that it begins, let it be borne
In such sort as may show our God, that we
Are faithful servants to his holy will.

EVE (pointing to CAIN)

His will!! the will of yon incarnate spirit
Of death, whom I have brought upon the earth
To strew it with the dead.   May all the curses
Of life be on him! and his agonies
Drive him forth o'er the wilderness,
From Eden, till his children do by him
As he did by his brother!   May the swords
And wings of fiery cherubim pursue him
By day and night—snakes spring up in his path—

Earth's fruits be ashes in his mouth—the leaves
On which he lays his head to sleep be strew'd
With scorpions! May his dreams be of his victim!
His waking a continual dread of death!
May the clear rivers turn to blood as he
Stoops down to stain them with his raging lip!
May every element shun or change to him!
May he live in the pangs which others die with
And death itself wax something worse than death
To him who first acquainted him with man!
Hence, fratricide! henceforth that word is *Cain*,
Through all the coming myriads of mankind,
Who shall abhor thee, though thou wert their sire!
May the grass wither from thy feet! the woods
Deny thee shelter! earth a home! the dust
A grave! the sun his light! and heaven her God! (18)

[*Exit* EVE.

ADAM

Cain! get thee forth: we dwell no more together.
Depart! and leave the dead to me—I am
Henceforth alone—we never must meet more. (19)

ADAH

Oh, part not with him thus, my father: do not
Add thy deep curse to Eve's upon his head!

ADAM

I curse him not: his spirit be his curse. (20)
Come, Zillah!

ZILLAH

I must watch my husband's corse.

ADAM

We will return again, when he is gone
Who hath provided for us this dread office.
Come, Zillah!

ZILLAH

Yet one kiss on yon pale clay,
And those lips once so warm—my heart! my heart!
　　　　　　　[*Exeunt* ADAM *and* ZILLAH *weeping*.

ADAH

Cain! thou hast heard, we must go forth. I am ready,
So shall our children be. I will bear Enoch,
And you his sister. Ere the sun declines
Let us depart, nor walk the wilderness
Under the cloud of night.—Nay, speak to me,
To *me—thine own*.

CAIN

Leave me!

ADAH

　　　　　　Why, all have left thee.

CAIN

And wherefore lingerest thou? Dost thou not fear
To dwell with one who hath done this?

ADAH

                              I fear
Nothing except to leave thee, much as I
Shrink from the deed which leaves thee brotherless.
I must not speak of this—it is between thee
And the great God.

A Voice from within exclaims,
                    Cain! Cain!

ADAH

                        Hear'st thou that voice?

The Voice within

Cain! Cain!

ADAH

                    It soundeth like an angel's tone.

Enter the ANGEL *of the Lord*

Where is thy brother Abel?

CAIN

                        Am I then
My brother's keeper?

ANGEL

                    Cain! what hast thou done?
The voice of thy slain brother's blood cries out,
Even from the ground, unto the Lord!—Now art thou
Cursed from the earth, which open'd late her mouth
To drink thy brother's blood from thy rash hand.

Henceforth, when thou shalt till the ground, it shall not
Yield thee her strength; a fugitive shalt thou
Be from this day, and vagabond on earth!

ADAH

This punishment is more than he can bear.
Behold, thou drivest him from the face of earth,
And from the face of God shall he be hid.
A fugitive and vagabond on earth,
'Twill come to pass, that whoso findeth him
Shall slay him.

CAIN

      Would they could! but who are they
Shall slay me? where are these on the lone earth
As yet unpeopled?

ANGEL

      Thou hast slain thy brother,
And who shall warrant thee against thy son?

ADAH

Angel of Light! be merciful, nor say
That this poor aching breast now nourishes
A murderer in my boy, and of his father.

ANGEL

Then he would but be what his father is.
Did not the milk of Eve give nutriment
To him thou now see'st so besmear'd with blood?

The fratricide might well engender parricides.—
But it shall not be so—the Lord thy God
And mine commandeth me to set his seal
On Cain, so that he may go forth in safety.
Who slayeth Cain, a sevenfold vengeance shall
Be taken on his head.   Come hither!

CAIN

What
Would'st thou with me?

ANGEL

To mark upon thy brow
Exemption from such deeds as thou hast done.

CAIN

No, let me die!

ANGEL

It must not be.
[*The* ANGEL *sets the mark on* CAIN'S *brow.*

CAIN

It burns
My brow, but nought to that which is within it.
Is there more? let me meet it as I may.

ANGEL

Stern hast thou been and stubborn from the womb,
As the ground thou must henceforth till; but he
Thou slew'st was gentle as the flocks he tended.

CAIN

After the fall too soon was I begotten;
Ere yet my mother's mind subsided from
The serpent, and my sire still mourn'd for Eden.
That which I am, I am; I did not seek
For life, nor did I make myself; but could I
With my own death redeem him from the dust—
And why not so? let him return to-day,
And I lie ghastly! so shall be restored
By God the life to him he loved: and taken
From me a being I ne'er loved to bear.

ANGEL

Who shall heal murder? what is done is done.
Go forth! fulfil thy days! and be thy deeds
Unlike the last!

　　　　　　　　　[*The* ANGEL *disappears.*

ADAH

　　　　He's gone, let us go forth;
I hear our little Enoch cry within
Our bower.

CAIN

　　　　Ah! little knows he what he weeps for!
And I who have shed blood cannot shed tears!

But the four rivers[1] would not cleanse my soul.
Think'st thou my boy will bear to look on me?

ADAH

If I thought that he would not, I would—

CAIN (*interrupting her*)

No,
No more of threats: we have had too many of them:
Go to our children; I will follow thee.

ADAH

I will not leave thee lonely with the dead;
Let us depart together.

CAIN

Oh! thou dead
And everlasting witness! whose unsinking
Blood darkens earth and heaven! what thou *now* art,
I know not! but if *thou* see'st what *I* am,
I think thou wilt forgive him, whom his God
Can ne'er forgive, nor his own soul.—Farewell!
I must not, dare not touch what I have made thee.
I, who sprung from the same womb with thee, drain'd
The same breast, clasp'd thee often to my own,
In fondness brotherly and boyish, I
Can never meet thee more, nor even dare

---

[1] The "four rivers" which flowed round Eden, and consequently the only waters with which Cain was acquainted upon the earth.

To do that for thee, which thou should'st have done
For me—compose thy limbs into their grave—
The first grave yet dug for mortality.
But who hath dug that grave? Oh, earth! Oh, earth!
For all the fruits thou hast render'd to me, I
Give thee back this.—Now for the wilderness.

     [ADAH *stoops down and kisses the body of* ABEL.

ADAH

A dreary, and an early doom, my brother,
Has been thy lot! Of all who mourn for thee,
I alone must not weep. My office is
Henceforth to dry up tears, and not to shed them;
But yet, of all who mourn, none mourn like me,
Not only for thyself, but him who slew thee.
Now, Cain! I will divide thy burden with thee.

CAIN

Eastward from Eden will we take our way;
'Tis the most desolate, and suits my steps.

ADAH

Lead! thou shalt be my guide, and may our God
Be thine! Now let us carry forth our children.

CAIN

And *he* who lieth there was childless. I
Have dried the fountain of a gentle race,
Which might have graced his recent marriage couch,

And might have temper'd this stern blood of mine,
Uniting with our children Abel's offspring!
O Abel!

ADAH

Peace be with him!

CAIN

But with *me!*——

[*Exeunt.*

THE END

Remarks

Philosophical and Critical

REMARKS

PHILOSOPHICAL AND CRITICAL

ACT I

(1) After what I have announced in my letter to Lord Byron, and in the preface that follows it, there remains nothing more to say concerning the basis of this Mystery. The reader has seen in what manner I have refused to Lord Byron the ground upon which he believed himself so firm, and how the reasons that he brings forward in his preface, reasons that he thought irresistible in the doctrine of his church, are overthrown in accordance with this same doctrine. I shall not return here to all that I have said, for this would be to repeat myself. Considering the substance of the poem as sufficiently refuted, since the author, in whatever manner he might reply, would enclose it in a syllogism or fall into absurdity, I shall be content with examining the forms; and I shall refute, as occasion shall present them, the subversive principles of morals and of social order that I believe to see laid down there, as well as the fatal consequences which might be deduced from them.

To begin by mingling praise with criticism: let us observe that if the intention of Lord Byron has been good in first presenting the primitive family as offering, at dawn, its homage to the Eternal, and if one cannot refuse to his lines the poetical beauty of admirable style, one is constrained to think, with Cain, that there is more of loudness than of veritable fervour in this morning prayer.

Adam and Eve evince no sentiment. That which Abel manifests, analogous to his weak and gentle character, shows a contradiction that Cain cannot fail to perceive. The shepherd who says that created beings people the worlds to enjoy them and to love one another, must unfortunately know that the greater part do not enjoy them without fear and that they scarcely love one another at all. For if his lambs, his bulls and his heifers love one another, the wolves and tigers that surround them do not act the same. Abel is here led by what he feels, but that which Cain thinks is opposed to him. Cold reason overthrows the edifice of a sentiment little reflected upon. Instead of saying that these beings live to love one another, Abel should have said that it is to love one another that they should live. Then Cain, naturally drawn to examine why that which ought to be is not, would come to discuss the cause of this contradiction; and by the very fact of admitting that what is not ought to be, he would give the victory to his brother. Abel, in saying that the thing is when it is not, opposes that which might be. In seeing the perfection, he arrests the perfectibility.

The idea contained in the prayer of Zillah is likewise false, and Lord Byron certainly knows it. He has purposely put it there to prepare for the violent departure of Cain. Zillah states as fact what is only in question. She says that God has permitted the serpent to profane Eden. If He had permitted it, the profanation would not have been for the serpent. For this being, whatever it may be, is too inferior to God to enjoy any independence with regard to the all-powerful Being. The serpent, however one may conceive of it, had done nothing but what Adam wished it to do; for Adam ruled in Eden. Everything had been put under his hand. If he had not ruled there, he would not have been responsible for anything. Zillah therefore, instead of speaking to God as author of the evil that she experiences, and instead of telling him, as she does, not to augment the evil, ought to pray Him, on the contrary, to lessen that which her parents had done, and which she continues to do herself. A sick man, suffering through his mistake does not call in a physician to augment his malady, but to cure it.

(2) The character, violent but always true, that Lord Byron gives to Cain, begins here to manifest itself. One has nothing with which to reproach him in this regard. Confining himself to the letter of the *Sepher*, he may in accordance with his doctrine, interpret this letter as he wishes; and after the manner in which he has conceived his *Dramatic Mystery*, the character of Cain must be as it is. But that with which he can be justly reproached, both as moralist and as poet, is having sacrificed to this character that of Adam, when he could have brought it out otherwise. I do not speak of the character of Abel; one can pardon his having weakened it as much as he could so as to diminish the enormity of the crime of Cain. But why leave Adam to play a rôle so insignificant? Here is an opportunity for him to reply to his rebellious son. He should not be lacking in reasons. Why should he leave this care to his wife, and

suffer her to throw his fault upon an insensible tree, so as to disencumber him thus of the fatal consequences with which Cain reproaches him?

The child who burns himself at the flame of a candle, accuses the incandescence of this flame, and often his complaisant mother or his stupid nurse enters into the falsity of this idea; nevertheless, does the weakness of the child or the nonsense of these women change the nature of things? Could the flame be luminous without being incandescent? The fire that decomposes the wax, and by a manner as secret as admirable, fills with light a place which, without this decomposition, would remain profoundly dark, is this fire guilty in burning? Must one curse it because it burns, because it has burned the finger of this child? Above all, should one curse the all-powerful, unfathomable Being to which it owes its origin? The child is burned, he suffers; does his evil come from the one who lighted the candle? It had been lighted to guide his steps, to divert his senses, to throw light upon his food, to befriend his play. But it was placed too near him . . .

This is the foolish thing that Lord Byron makes his poor Adam pronounce: "Oh God! why didst Thou plant the tree of knowledge?"

Why? to give thee, insensate one, the knowledge of the things that thou needest to know; to give it to thee little by little as thou shalt be able to bear it. But thou goest on listening to the voice of an insidious passion and the inclination of a will preoccupied with its own importance, urging thee to gather this fruit of knowledge which is still green and bitter; thou, still young and weak, thou art not in condition to bear it and because thine intemperance hurts thee, thou murmurest! Wert thou not warned of the harm that would come from touching it?

Yes; but why not render its harmfulness to me impossible?

It is certain that by tying up the child of which I have just spoken, he would not burn himself at the candle; but also he would not develop himself; and if his state of restraint lasted very long, he would stifle.

(3) Again it is the time for making Adam speak; but Lord Byron has certainly felt that he must determine either to give him some force or to condemn him to silence. He has condemned him to silence and has given the speech to Eve, who uses it with her usual skill, without touching the real point of the difficulty, and consistently rejecting her fault concerning exterior things. Once it was a fatal tree which had borne bitter fruit; now it is a snare that has caused their ruin. She praises to Cain the resignation of his father; she invites him to imitate his example. But resignation is not in the character of Cain. It is not by sending him to labour and exhorting him to silence that one can satisfy his reason. He had laid down a question frank and decisive: he had asked, since life and knowledge are equally good, what evil could there be in living and in knowing? It was to this that he wanted an answer. Adam alone was in a position to give it. Why did he not do so? It is the secret of Lord Byron. The poet held his personages in his hands; it depended only upon him to give the speech to whom he would. Let us still respect his secret, but endeavour to supply his silence.

But before approaching this delicate subject, I must again inform the reader that I speak here in the meaning of the *Dramatic Mystery of Cain*, and that I see human personages where the author sees them. After having ousted him from his ground, I allow him peacefully to replace himself there, to show him that even from the point of view whence he considers his primitive family, he has misplaced the principles that should rule it. It is no longer a question here of cosmogony, but of morals and of social order.

Now what was the question Cain asked of his father? He asked him how it is possible that to live and have knowledge is evil; and what reasons could the Eternal have for refusing man knowledge and life? Adam, instead of replying to this, allows his wife to declaim and afterward sends his son to labour. This conduct necessarily sours the mind of Cain, irritates him and prepares all that follows in the drama. One feels indeed that Lord Byron makes too great a sacrifice here to the interest of his poetry. Never in nature can things happen thus. A father, in the situation in which Adam finds himself, interrogated by his son, would certainly reply if he could; and if he could not, he would frankly declare his ignorance. He would be careful not to let his wife, with idle and ridiculous declamations, fill the mind of his son with phantoms, and persuade him that a tyrannical decree, imposed without motive and without design, is the cause of all the evils they suffer. Let us suppose that Adam, instructed in the truth, replies to his son; this is what he would say:

"Life and knowledge are equally good; but they require to be suitably united, and in proportion to one another.

Although a child may enjoy life from the moment of his birth, his life, still weak and as it were at its dawn, has not enough vigour to resist the commotions of body and of soul that later it can support. If one considers this child in the matter of food, one sees that he has need only for a light milk; and that, if one gave him anything else, if one tried to nourish him in the same manner as a man, it would inevitably kill him. That which holds for the body, holds likewise for the soul. If it experiences the shocks of strong passions too early, it succumbs to them. It is the same with the mind. Knowledge which is its portion, should be given it with precaution. Wishing that a child should know in his tender youth what he ought to know only when he has arrived at manhood, is to lose him."

After Adam had said these words to his son Cain, seeing that Cain admitted the premises, although he might still not conceive the application clearly, he would add:

"The Eternal God, my son, gave life and knowledge to man; but life in the flower of its adolescence, and knowledge only in germ. He willed that the one should be developed after the other, and that they should come together at their highest degree of fullness and perfection. Man knew that it was so, and even that it could only be so. He knew that a precocious knowledge would expose his life, and could even ravish it from him. As to what this absence of life called *death* is, he had only a confused idea. All that he comprehended was that it was a redoubtable state.

"Now a fatal event having put all knowledge within my reach, I could not resist the desire of possessing it. It is useless to give thee an account of it, because it can only be

considered by thee in its results; thou canst not comprehend
it in its principle because thou art still only a child. Drawn
on by blind passion and thinking to escape the danger with
which I was menaced, I seized the fruit that was offered me.
My audacity took precedence of time; my mind, in fact,
usurped knowledge. But the prediction of the Eternal God
was accomplished; my life, too weak, succumbed beneath
the weight with which I had overwhelmed it. It could no
longer grow; it was obliged to decline. An eternal decline
is the most horrible of sufferings. The Eternal God saved
me from it, by vouchsafing to change the mode of my life.
Then thou wert born. Without the event of which I have
just told thee, thou wouldst not have been born, Eve would
not be thy mother, thy brother would not have seen the
light of day, and all humanity which shall be born of you,
would not exist." Adam would cease at these words, and
leave Cain to his reflections.

(4) If Cain had reflected properly upon what I have
supposed Adam might have said to him, his soul, instead
of being more and more irritated as it was by the discourses
of his mother, would have been calmed. The force of his
reason, instead of acting incessantly upon itself and involving
itself in a whirl of ideas, specious, but contrary to truth,
would have acted upon exterior things, and submitted to
them. Then this power of the will, this grandeur of character which was sent forth on the course of error and drove Cain
to his perdition, would have exercised itself no longer except
for good, and would have made him the greatest of all men.
But it was necessary that it happen otherwise, so that Lord

Byron might be able to give us his *Dramatic Mystery*.

I can not blame the noble English poet for having followed the vulgar tradition which condemns Cain to bear the abominable name of fratricide, since, in short, this tradition exists; but I do blame him for having made everything around this unfortunate one conspire to force him to this detestable act. I say that such a dramatic course is bad; it is contrary to the nature of things, to morals and to truth. There should have been given, as I have shown, a counterpoise to the animistic passion by which Cain is allured, so as to establish a combat in his very soul, between truth and error. This combat would certainly have brought about poetical beauties of the highest order, that Lord Byron was well capable of feeling and depicting. Moreover, nothing would have hindered him from at last making Cain incline to the part of crime; and then the personage of Lucifer would have become really dramatic. In the position in which he has put him, his rôle is limited to violent declamations, of which Cain has no need, and in which one sees that the infernal spirit expresses himself by habit rather than by necessity.

But let us suppose, although Lord Byron has not said it, that Cain should be more stirred by the passionate narrations of his mother than by the cold and deliberate reasonings of his father; that he should still see the downfall of his parents as caused by exterior things which did not depend upon circumstances they could have avoided; that he should continue to be irritated both against those unknown things, the idea of which mastered him, and against the all-powerful Being, even more unknown, which, according to him, had prepared these things to bring about evil in the world; what would have been his speech in this case?

It would have been as that of men whom I call volitive, men matured by their will alone, who ever murmur against destiny, ever are unable to recognize Providence, or, identifying it with themselves, render it responsible for their own thought. The language of Cain would have been nearly that which the English poet has put into his mouth, and which he has copied from the discourses, more or less virulent, that he has heard a thousand times in all classes of society; fatal discourses, but unfortunately too common, which I have heard as well as he, and which any man who associates more or less with his fellow-men can recall having heard. As the men who use this language are numerous, the public morals are in danger. Religion consists only of vain ceremonies; force alone submits the governed to the governors; even family ties are broken; everything is individuated, and the most terrible revolutions brood secretly beneath the débris of revolutions. If it were possible that this language should become universal, the universe would be menaced with total subversion.

(5) Cain, relying only upon his own thought, and receiving only laws of his own, personifies and represents in a single being the volitive spirit in its greatest exaltation. This spirit, which Lord Byron calls Lucifer, differs not really from Cain. It is the spirit itself of Cain, which, being reflected as in a magic mirror, is presented to him under the traits of a distinct being. But in order for us to conform to the idea of the English poet and to the vulgar tradition of

which he renders himself interpreter, let us consent to see here a real being, the genius of evil, Satan, the devil; and let us give him the name of Lucifer, since it agrees with Lord Byron to name him thus. But, in conforming to this idea, I do not pretend either to forget or to abandon what I said in my introductory letter, that this personage has never been known by Moses as a distinct, independent being.

The dogma of the downfall of the rebellious angels does not enter in any way into the cosmogony of the lawgiver of the Hebrews; and whether that theodoxical writer may have been ignorant or not of this dogma, at least it is very certain that he did not admit it. The Jews, from whom we have it, received it from the ancient Chaldeans still inhabiting Assyria; and the latter owed it to the disciples of the first Zoroaster. What gave birth to this dogma was an old cosmogonical tradition of the Hindus. In it one learned that the genii of the north and of the south of the earth had been divided, ever since the origin of the world, on the subject of the beverage of immortality, of which they pretended equally to conserve the exclusive possession. This division brought about long and disastrous combats, the result of which was the complete overthrow of the genii of the south, called *Assours*, and their subjugation by those of the north, named *Devas*. This tradition, which one also finds in almost the same terms in the *Edda* of the Scandinavians, was known by the Egyptians, the Greeks and the Romans as the *War of the Gods against the Giants*.

But, without engaging ourselves further in these cosmogonic details, which I have declared I would not enter into here, let us conclude that in receiving the dramatic personage whom Lord Byron presents to us under the name of Lucifer, we do not pretend in any way to link it to the doctrine of Moses, which remains foreign here.

Moreover, Lord Byron, in describing this personage, recalls the ideas of Milton; but he is far from surpassing them.

(6) I pray the reader to observe that Lucifer does not deviate here from the idea that I expressed at the beginning of the preceding article, and that he allows it to be understood clearly enough that he is only a sort of magic reflection of the spirit of Cain, reacted upon by an astral power.

(7) Cain takes refuge in the idea that I have put into the mouth of Adam; he says that, by too great precipitation, the tree of knowledge has been stripped of its fruit before its maturity. This is remarkable. As Plato says, poets sometimes know the truth by a sort of intuition.

(8) Lucifer discloses here a great mystery to Cain, according to the word of Lord Byron, who praises himself in his preface for it. He teaches him that the power of death does not extend over all his being, and that the most noble part of himself, his soul, is immortal. Doubtless, if the matter stood thus, all mankind could not but render thanks to Lucifer for such an admirable discovery. The sectarians called Ophites, or Serpentinians, would have been right to accord him a cult under the form of the serpent; and those called Cainites could not be blamed for having regarded Cain as patriarch *par excellence* and the saviour of the world.

For, consider that as there can be nothing new under the sun, the idea of the English poet, inferring that it is Satan or the devil who has been the instructor of men, the good and helpful being who has drawn them out from the state of ignorance into which the Creator of the world had put them and willed maliciously to keep them there; consider, I say, that this idea, wholly bizarre as it appears, is not new.

The Ophites made it the basis of their belief, and the Cainites, who had adopted it, proclaimed themselves descendants of Cain. In him they personified knowledge, strength, grandeur of soul, and all the virtues of man; and in Abel, on the contrary, ignorance, weakness, cowardice and all the vices which come therefrom. Consequently they regarded the murder of Abel as having been favourable to humanity, and said that there would have been no other way of preventing ignorance and imbecility from dominating the earth; that they would necessarily have dominated, if the race of Abel had not been stifled in its origin. They said that it was quite enough for the race of Seth to have propagated among men the weakness of character, the pusillanimity that delivers them to slavery, the ignorance of the soul and the superstitious terrors of the mind that carry them to fanaticism. It was to avoid all these consequences, which appear to come from the vulgar meaning given to the first chapters of *Genesis*, that Marcion made up his mind to reject this holy book entirely; and perhaps it was, as I have said in my letter to Lord Byron, to avoid in future the troubles that these opinions had caused, that the Christian church adopted the wise resolution of forbidding its reading by the people.

God forbid, however, that I should believe that the author of the *Mystery of Cain* had a plan to renew the errors of the Ophites and the Cainites, whom he has probably never heard mentioned; but although his intention has not been such, his work tends that way none the less, from beginning to end. It is above all in the passage where I stopped the reader, that the poet, establishing the existence of two principles, evidently confounds their attributes. He gives to the Creator of the world the evil intention of keeping man in the ignorance to which he had created him, without revealing to him the goal of his existence, which is immortality. Contrariwise, he gives to his antagonist, Lucifer, in the work of creation, the praiseworthy design of making man emerge from that state of darkness and dependance, in causing the light of knowledge, of liberty and of eternal life to shine before his eyes.

In order that the reasoning of the Ophites might be even seemingly right, and that their doctrine, put in beautiful lines by Lord Byron, might be sustained, it would have been necessary first of all, not to state as fact that which is in question; and not only just to say that the intention of the Creator of the world was to leave man in ignorance so as to hold him in servitude, but to prove it. The reasoning of these sectarians would not differ from that of a domestic animal if he could reason and act.

A hunting dog, for example, seeing his master's child held in leading strings, watched over, kept from eating food that he himself ate, prevented from doing the things that he did, put away from a thousand things, and above all strongly admonished every time he wished to take hold of a sharp instrument, or even to reach out an arm to the fire, would conclude that this child was in shameful slavery, in crass ignorance, that one wished to ravish all his rights from him and prevent him from being a powerful man, a vigorous huntsman or a warrior useful to his country. Then if this dog, also with good intention, approached the child, and tried to make him feel the odious tyranny under which he lived; if he stuffed him secretly with the meats that had been thrown to him for his nourishment, so as to make him grow rapidly; and if he persuaded him to seize the weapons of his father to go to the chase with him, do you not believe that it would kill the child, and that it would expose him even to the danger of killing others?

See what, in place of the English poet, who had not thought of it, I have made Adam say in my third *Remark*. The Creator of the world had not denied either knowledge or life to Adam, since He had given the principles of both to him. He had only willed that these principles should be developed together, and be nourished gradually and mutually. This course, which was that of the nature He had already created, was thus determined by His divine Providence, a living law, irrefragable and immutable as It. This course having been inverted by an event, possible but by no means forced, the nature of Adam was altered by a malady which momentarily changed the mode of his life. The effect of this malady, retrograding in eternity, could only be cured by a remedy called *time;* a remedy prepared beforehand, and possible in the same manner as the event which had caused the downfall of this universal man.

(9) Lucifer says further on, in the scene where he replies
to Adah,[1] that he aided the Creator in the work of creation;
which contradicts a little what he advances here, without
however, destroying it wholly. For it can be understood
that, whereas he aided, he would have wished to do the work
alone. But the contradiction can not disappear without
letting appear a difficulty still greater. It is this: that if
Lucifer, at the moment when he wished to create the world,
was obliged to aid the One who created it, he recognized, in
obeying, that this Creator was not only his subjugator, but
his superior; which he emphatically denies, nevertheless,
several times.

(10) Here is a singular reflection that the English poet
has put into the mouth of Satan. He makes him say that
he, Satan, does not know, and above all does not believe,
that the Creator has made the things as He says; that is to
say, as He has been made to say in the *Bible*. This could
corroborate all that I have taken the liberty to explain to
Lord Byron in the letter that I have written pertaining to
the three meanings contained in the original of this ancient
and mysterious book, of which one alone, the literal and
material meaning, has been rendered by the Hellenist translators. But if the English noble knew this immense difficulty,
if he knew only that it might be possible for the thought of
Moses not to be rendered in the imperfect copies that we
have of his *Sepher*, what becomes of all the anti-providential
declamations with which the poet has filled his *Dramatic
Mystery?* What becomes of all the consequences he has

[1] Act I, *Remark* 37.

pretended to draw from principles which he destroys here in a single word?

(11) Gratuitous impiety in the mouth of Satan, which nothing has yet justified. It is necessary that this volitive spirit be considered as profoundly identified with the soul of Cain, to dare hazard before him such assertions, without supporting them by the slightest proof.

(12) Vain and odious declamations, in which one finds only gigantic ideas, piling one upon another without foundation, like vapours that escape from a volcano. There is herein no point that merits being mentioned. All that can be distinguished through the blackish clouds and the sulphurous lightnings that furrow this discourse is the incommensurable grandeur of the Being of whom Lucifer speaks, and the terror His unalterable majesty causes him. Let us remark, in passing, that if this is the *spiritual politeness*, within the limits of which the noble poet promised, in his preface, to restrict the audacity of Lucifer, this politeness has something striking. One would say that this haughty spirit is here polite unwittingly. But, however, if it is thus for Lucifer, it is not the same for Lord Byron, who assuredly is not a poet unwittingly. His poetry here is admirable. One only regrets seeing it so badly employed. All this passage is of a frightful sublimity in the original.

(13) A new proof of what I have said in the fifth *Remark;* that Lucifer differs really not from Cain, of whom he is only a poetic reflection. In listening to Satan, Cain believes he hears himself speaking.

(14) The sympathy Cain experiences is quite natural after what has been said. His discourse is only a sort of repetition of the preceding one, already refuted in the fourth *Remark*. The poet again copies what he daily hears said by those volitive men who, in all classes, wearied by the necessity of destiny, find nothing in the promises of Providence which can soften the bitternesses of life. Accustomed to make themselves the centre, and to see the universe reflected in their person, they cannot be offended in the least of their sentiments, cannot feel the least of their will repulsed by other wills, or be arrested by natural obstacles dependent upon fortune, without accusing Providence, without regarding the divine laws as suspended, and universal harmony as troubled. If they are happy, they are astonished that the sky is covered with clouds; and if they weep, that all nature does not go into mourning. They are like those peasants of whom a certain novelist writes, who, victims of a fire which, during the night and by their fault, had ravaged their village, seated in the morning upon the sad débris of their cottages, were surprised that, despite their sorrow, the sun should again rise in the east to light the universe.

As to the description that Cain gives of his family, it is such as it pleases the poet to sketch, such as is fitting for him to show to the reader in his *Dramatic Mystery;* but it is certainly not such as nature would have given, if ever a similar family had found itself in like circumstances. The weakest character, that of Adam, is precisely the one that ought to be the strongest. I am sorry that Lord Byron did not put himself in a position to feel it better. He was capable with the fine talent with which nature has endowed him, to depict it properly. Before him, Milton had also failed; but he did not fail for the same reasons.

(15) I have promised in the *Remarks upon Lord Byron's Preface* to note the passages in which Lucifer sings truly upon the lyre of our poet. This passage is worthy of attention; not only is it true, but it is also perfectly moral.

(16) One moment, Lord Lucifer. One does not ask you if you have spoken true or false. One asks you if you have tempted; that is to say, if you have spoken the truth with perfidious intention and in a moment when it ought not to have been spoken. For this is precisely what you have done, by your own confession. Were Adam there, and if he conserved the least force of reasoning, he would easily show you that it is in vain for you to try to make fall on the Creator of the world, a fault that you two partook of together,— you for having inspired it, and he, Adam, for having committed it.

Since I have ventured already to supply the silence of the poet who has put you into the scene, by making Adam speak, allow me again to take the same liberty. Let us suppose that it was to this father of mankind that you addressed yourself instead of to his son. This is what he would have replied to you:

"You know that life, which I enjoy and you enjoy, existed before me, and even before you. You know that the beings who come here by the will of the One who is Master, whether, in effect, He has created it, as He said, or whether it has created itself, as you pretend; you know, I say, that these beings do not enjoy life at first in all its fullness. I have heard you declare that you knew beings, now infinite, who, in their finite origin, had been as weak as I; whereas others, formerly very powerful, have diminished in force and are even extinct in space. Do you not acknowledge this?"

You could not, Lucifer, deny these premises, without making your poet lie, who has precisely announced them by your mouth and in the same terms.[1] You should acknowledge this. Adam continues:

"Now, if you know this, you also know that when I arrived at life, I was weak and feeble, although destined to become very strong and very great, if I had been able to await the magnificent developments that the Eternal God had attached to my destinies. Having entered into life as into the dawn of a beautiful day, I ought to have followed its phases, and nourished myself from the marvellous tree of knowledge, in proportion as the strength of my life would permit me to digest its fruits. Still far from that moment, I knew that I could not approach it, and not only that the fruits were not ripe in my Eden, but that my spirit was too feeble to support the spirituous intoxication.

"The Eternal God, you know it, had created me in the image of the gods. But you also know, and I have heard you say it in your fits of passion against Him, that He is the sole unlimited, the indissoluble One[2]; and that, in consequence, the gods, or, as otherwise called, angels, interior spirits like you, or exterior spirits like Gabriel, are mutable. I was therefore mutable like them, and limited besides in the feebleness of spiritual adolescence. The Eternal, in

[1] Act II, *Rem.* 10.   [2] Act I, *Rem.* 12.

building my Eden, had well secured me from exterior attacks, but it was for me to secure myself from interior attacks; and for this I had sufficient strength and all possible instructions. My Creator Himself had enlightened me upon the sole danger that I might incur, and His angels came daily to support my weakness.

"However, as interior spirit, and the greatest of interior spirits, you had entered into my Eden. You were necessary there, you, called *Lucifer* by those who love you, *Satan* by those who love you not, and by me, who neither love you nor hate you, *Nahash*, the name that was given you in your origin.[1] You were necessary there because, without you, it would have been impossible for me to acquire any volitive force, and to attain, in consequence, to any of my animistic developments. It is justly, therefore, that you say you aided the Creator in the work of creation[2]; this is true, and your rôle was fine enough for you to have been contented with it. But, because the Eternal God had made you an interior spirit, you aspired to be an exterior spirit, perhaps to be both at the same time, which is incompatible; and you trusted, by reuniting the two opposed faculties, to concen-

---

[1] The name Lucifer signifies *light-bearer*. This name has been given to him because of a poetic exclamation of Isaiah, which appeared to make allusion to him, and which calls him הילל בן־שׁחר (*Hillel ben-shahar*), the resplendant one, son of darkness; a name that has been translated as *Lucifer, son of the morning*. This has made it become confused with the star of the morning, of which Lucifer is the Latin name. The name *Satan*, which is given him by Job, signifies in Hebrew שׂטן, that which is bent down, inclined, distant from another thing, opposed, contrary. This word is attached to the name we give to the south pole, which we regard also as inclined, and contrary in this respect to the north pole. It is not out of place to say here that Moses often takes the name *Satan* in the good sense, and even applies it to the angels of light. As to the name *Nahash*, I have explained it in my letter to Lord Byron.

[2] Act I, *Rem.* 37.

trate in yourself the two principles of the universe, and to become equal to or even to surpass the Most High.

"Look at me, *Nahash;* and see if I indeed know you. You thought that to succeed in this bold design, it was necessary for you to take possession of an exterior spirit still in its adolescence, so that it would offer you less difficulty to seize, and might afterward, in being developed under your laws, serve you as a fulcrum to attain to the principle of which you desired possession. I can not say that your intention was precisely to do me evil, for you were absolutely ignorant of what the result of your enterprise would be; and at present, even, though you have seen it, you are still ignorant of it, because you throw upon my inexperience and upon my foolishness, that which has been the effect of an inevitable destiny. You believe, as I understand it,[1] that I might have been able to seize the two principles at once and strip both the tree of knowledge and that of life; but you are in error. I could not take possession of the one, without the other being taken from me forever. Such was the eternal decree unchanged from the origin of things.

"In persuading me to lay hands upon the tree of knowledge, you unconsciously confounded error with truth; and you tempted me in this point, that you offered me as real a future that was illusory. Nevertheless, I will not declaim against you, as I hear my Eve sometimes declaim. It is too easy to throw upon alien things the fault of which one is himself guilty. I must say that I alone was guilty, since, with whatever force you were armed, I was strong enough to resist you, if I had willed it. I will even admit that in tempt-

[1] Act I, *Rem.* 3, 18.

ing me by magnificent promises, you did not deceive me as much as you were yourself deceived, and that you were as surprised as I was, in seeing that the knowledge of which I took possession, instead of pushing my life ahead into eternity, threw it backward, and exposed me to a catastrophe that neither you nor I could arrest. The Eternal God alone had that power. It was then that I saw what you can not see, and that I understood what you can not understand: the vanity of your undertakings."

(17) Adam has replied beforehand to this new attack of Lucifer; and he has done it with great moderation. He has not accused this spirit of having willed to ruin him; he has only shown that he acted with ignorance and presumption. This defect on the one side and excess on the other, again mislead Lucifer, and precipitate him into the same course. He believes he can do with Cain what he was unable to do with Adam, and succeed in taking possession of the two principles. But here the difficulty is augmented, since Adam, in a new mode of existence, is already divided and reflected in two beings, whose characters differ essentially. Lucifer feels very clearly that he cannot act equally upon both, and that it is necessary first to destroy the one by the other. Cain offers him a means that he seizes with eagerness, and by means of which, being identified with him, he drives him to the murder of his brother.

Here the situation of the son of Adam becomes frightful. Led to fratricide by ways of which he can absolutely neither understand nor avoid the goal, he goes on without willing it, without forseeing it, drawn along by an irresistible power.

Nothing around him enlightens him, nothing keeps him back; everything conspires in favour of the crime that he is about to commit. This is the radical fault of this drama, its danger and its immorality.

In order to render it moral and to remove its dangers, the poet should have thought of doing what the ancient poets did in similar circumstances. He should have admitted a choir of angels, an invisible and aërial choir who would have warned Cain of his situation, and would have thrown enough light upon his steps so that his conduct might not be entirely forced. The ancients derived a great advantage from this moral personage that they called *choir*, as can be seen in the tragedies that remain to us of the Greek theatre. The moderns, who have thought proper to take up the same subjects, have fallen into grave difficulties, as can be seen in *Œdipus*, and even in *Phædra*.

The discourses of Adam that I have been obliged to introduce into my *Remarks*, take the place of this choir, of which I am sorry Lord Byron had not thought. That would have rendered his drama moral, and would have facilitated the theatrical production, which, I believe, would have had a great effect if it had taken place.

(18) See the two preceding *Remarks*.

(19) Lucifer here discloses his essence to Cain, who gives no attention, so much is he occupied with his own ideas. This essence is derived from the volitive principle, one of the three great principles which rule the universe. The other two are Providence and Destiny. I have spoken very ex-

haustively of these three principles in my work *l'Etat social de l'Homme,*[1] and I have tried, as much as was possible for me, to make them understood and to show their reciprocal influence in the divers governments. I pray the reader to consider that I do not say Lucifer is the volitive principle, but only that he is derived from it and that his essence comes therefrom. One can, besides, review what I have said in the fourth and twelfth *Remarks*.

(20) What Lucifer says here is amphibological, as is all that which he continues to say. What he constantly means, yet veils with obscure words, is that he has not tempted Adam, since it is not in him to speak the truth. Adam replied to this in the sixteenth *Remark*.

(21) Lucifer defends himself forcibly against ever having taken the form of a serpent. Indeed, there is nothing in the sacred book that indicates it. After having hesitated to disclose to Cain what he ought to understand by this mysterious serpent, he finishes by telling him in proper terms. He teaches him that the spirit which tempted Adam was in him and that he only awakened it. This ought to be a ray of light for Cain, who, however, takes no heed, allured as he is by this same spirit which already usurps all his faculties.

(22) After identifying himself with the spirit of Cain, and stirring his passions, Lucifer strikes his imagination, and draws it adroitly along to the most terrible idea that could agitate it,—death.

---

[1] *Hermeneutic Interpretation of the Origin of the Social State of Man.* Fabre d'Olivet, Putnam, N. Y.

(23) It is certainly not to this that Adam ought to be limited. To say only that death is frightful is to say nothing about it. But it was a means taken by our noble poet to weaken the character of this father of mankind. Without that, his *Dramatic Mystery* would not have been able to sustain itself. For ourselves, we have not the same interest. We shall speak later of it. Let us leave Cain to rave for a moment; and also Lucifer, who with vague, insignificant words excites more and more the terror that brings him to this raving.

(24) Lucifer must reckon much upon the preoccupation into which he has thrown his interlocutor, in order to dare say to him, without bringing to bear the slightest proof, that the Creator of the world makes but to destroy. Now what does He destroy? The bodies no doubt. But He does not destroy them. He frees them to new formations; and the spirit which animates them, unalterable in its essence, elaborates itself in this movement. It is healed thus, by means of time, of that fatal malady of which Adam, who was its author and victim, has spoken several times.[1] Why does not the master of spirits know this? Where is the immense knowledge of which he boasts?[2]

(25) For the master of spirits, for the one who claims to know all, this is a very poor reply. Death is, according to him, a return to earth; or, as his interpreter says, death consists of being *resolved into the earth*. It seems to me that if Adam had been questioned as closely upon this matter, he

[1] Act I, *Rem.* 3 and 16.
[2] Idem., *Rem.* 26.

would not have replied thus. We shall see it a little further on; something must be kept for the second Act.

(26) This is vain boasting, as I have already remarked. If Lucifer knows all, might he not show it by telling what death is?

(27) Cain experiences a movement of doubt which might have led him far, if he had been given the time to ponder upon it. The English poet, despite his partiality, has been unable to prevent one from feeling here the weakness of this master of spirits, who calls himself great, superb, adored by legions of spirits, and who finds himself, nevertheless, forced to recoil before the obstinate pride of a man. This man acts here in his proper essence, and without perceiving it, profits against his instructor by the counsel that this instructor had given him for another purpose, in saying to him:

> By being
> Yourselves, in your resistance. Nothing can
> Quench the mind, if the mind will be itself
> And centre of surrounding things—'tis made
> To sway.

A great mystery is no doubt contained in these words. To explain it here is impossible; but I have made very great efforts in another work[1] to show all its consequences in the political destinies of the universe.

(28) Lucifer, who had been obliged to give way for a moment before the genius of Cain, which was on the point

[1] *Hermeneutic Interpretation of the Origin of the Social State of Man.* Fabre d'Olivet.

of being awakened, recovers himself here, and resumes his superiority. The reply that he makes to Cain upon the question of knowing how, by not adoring the Eternal, one gives oneself to Lucifer, contains a reticence very bitter. One cannot conceive why the son of Adam does not feel that the necessity of a frightful destiny is here founded in principle. It is true that if he felt it, the drama would have finished there; and this is not the design of the poet, who, in order to continue it, has need to throw Cain into a new divagation.

(29) Lord Byron follows here the system of the rabbis who assert that, in the first ages of the world, all confinements were double; that is to say, that women always gave birth to two children at a time, the one male and the other female. These two, nourished and brought up together, were destined by Providence to become husband and wife, and to procreate in the same manner new twins. This order of things ceased when the world was sufficiently peopled; and it was forbidden for a brother and sister, born alternately of the same mother, to unite together. One finds no trace of this system in the writings of Moses. I shall not dwell on this subject.

(30) What perfidious and insidious words! Now that Lucifer is sure of Cain, he attacks Adah, and attacks her on the side where he knows she will be most accessible, where she will give most attention, and will be most easily moved. He brings her to think of love; he makes her uneasy concerning the future fate of her children, frightens her concerning the purity of her union with Cain, makes her foresee a crime

in the future; brings her back to love, and makes her consider what the effect of knowledge is upon this sentiment. Here his reasonings are very narrow, and designedly filled with an obscurity which seems to render them stronger.

The Eternal God, according to him, can only be loved as long as He is not known; and this is why He puts so much importance upon withholding knowledge from the hearts of His adorers, and keeping them deep in ignorance. The crime of Adam was in leaving that ignorance, in spite of Him. This father of men was unable, according to the reasoning of Lucifer, to acquire knowledge without losing love; but as he does not find himself strong enough to testify boldly to his hatred, by walking openly in the steps of Satan; and as the power of his Master has struck him with terror, he gives by fear what he can no longer give by love, and adores Him through fear.

It is impossible, one feels it plainly, for Adah to reply to a reasoning so infernal. The only sentiment she feels is fright. She takes refuge in the arms of Cain. But Cain, far from sustaining her, abandons her to her enemy, by making her clearly understand that what Lucifer has just said with regard to Adam would be equally true for him, if the force of his soul did not shelter him from fear. He tells her that, as for him, he loves absolutely nothing but her, that is to say, only himself in her; that he yields to a blind, thoughtless sentiment, a passion which impels him; but that, beyond this passion and the objects that it can encompass, he is indifferent.

It would be fitting if a loving being took the right to

speak here. The choir of angels of which I have spoken would now be perfectly in its place. In default of this choir, let us once again call Adam into the scene, and let us suppose that he has heard the discourse of Satan. This is what he would say:

"Stop, *Nahash;* you absolutely confuse things, and following your custom, you mix truth with error. It is not true that I adore the Eternal God through fear; I adore Him through recognition! I can not deny that the love I bear today for this great Being differs from that which I bore for Him in Eden; you would assume too much advantage over me if I dared to say the contrary. My love in Eden was pure and simple as I was. It was a sentiment mingled with my life, which did not appear to me as distinct being. I could not have ceased to love, even though I had willed it. Love was as the principle of my being, and the light of my life.

" Now, on the contrary, my being has become its principle, and my life is detached from it. I know as a free sentiment that which I knew only as a mode of existence. Now, I admit, fear is mingled with it. I have experienced a sort of religious terror in considering the immensity of the Being I was permitted to love without reflection, and as a child loves its mother. I have seen my father in Him, my father offended. I have loved Him with reserve and timidity. But it is in vain that you take the fear and even the terror, of which I have just spoken, for the sentiments with which this great Being inspires me. No, you deceive yourself. You borrow for me your own sensations; but, *Nahash,* your sentiments are not mine.

" Reflect upon this: our positions, although alike in certain respects, differ nevertheless essentially. For that which I have become, I ought not to be; and you, you ought to be that which you have become. The fear and the terror that I feel, it is myself who gives them to me. These are the sentiments which are within me, and which come out, not from a source of truth, but from a false source that my mistake has opened. Now that my divine love has become a free sentiment, I fear lest I have not enough, and I dread lest I have too much. Strive to understand me, *Nahash;* and feel, if possible, how an adoration can be mingled with fear, and how a religious terror can be mingled with love.

"But I speak of things which are foreign to you. I will endeavour another time, in taking up the sequel of this discourse, to speak to you less of my sentiments and perhaps more of yours than you would wish."

(31) Always a repetition of the same ideas; always stating as fact that which is in question; always the same exaltation of the volitive principle that nothing can temper. Lucifer at least reasons; but Cain reasons not. He precipitates himself violently into the redoubtable road which is open to him. His own will, which he has been told is irrefragable in its sovereignty, makes itself the centre of everything, gives itself as the measure of everything, and demands that everything be related to it. It sees nothing but itself and that which touches, flatters or frightens it; and forgetting that it is in the universe, encloses the universe in itself. It is astonished that there should be other laws than those which it might claim to dictate. This discourse, as those of the

same nature that I have refuted,[1] is only the copy of discourses more or less violent or bitter that one hears against
Providence in all classes of society by volitive men whose
religion does not temper their character.

(32) This is an interpellation to which Adah is utterly
unable to reply. Lucifer here gives proof of ignorance, if
indeed he does not give proof of bad faith. He plays upon
the word *alone*. But the word *alone*, in speaking of a human
individual, has not the same meaning it has in speaking of
the Being of beings. A man *alone* is not a man *unique*. One
can not apply to immensity, to infinity, to eternity, the
same expressions that one attaches to individuality, to quan-
tity, to limited time, and draw the same inductions therefrom, without falling into absurdity. Lucifer here falls into
it knowingly or unknowingly. God, not being a finite and
limited individual, can never be *alone* in the sense in which
one understands it for a man. The universe itself, which is
only an image, very imperfect and very remote, of God, is
not *alone* in the same sense. There is no need of company
to be good, and still less to be happy.

(33) It is not necessary to carry the question so high,
Lucifer, to know why you are not from heaven. Adam is
sufficient to reply to that; he has already replied[2] in saying
to you yourself that you are an interior spirit. It is true
you are the first of these spirits, and the most eminently
necessary to the work of creation, holding, by your essence,

[1] Act I, *Rem.* 4, 5, 14.
[2] Act I, *Rem.* 16.

to one of the great principles of the universe, but alien to
the celestial intelligences.   Could it be that Adam knew you
better than you knew yourself, Lucifer, or at least better
than your poet knew you?

(34) You say, Lucifer, that you have resisted? It pleases
you to say that. Adam assures that you have only had the
intention of resisting; and that it was for the purpose of
giving yourself an auxiliary in this projected combat that
you induced him, by illusory promises, to pluck unseasonably
the fruit of knowledge.

(35) The "reason" you advocate unceasingly, do you
understand it well, Lucifer? It seems to me that you take
it for a principle, for a cause, whereas it is only a consequence,
only an effect; it is a passive instrument that you transform
into an active motive. It guides the artisan in his work, but
it does not do the work. The lyre must needs be in tune;
but if it is played by an ignorant, unskilled or mocking
musician, it will render only a false harmony. It is also
necessary, without doubt, that it be in tune so that the best
musician may make use of it. All its merit is limited to being
in tune. It is, after all, indifferent to every kind of melody.
Reason is like a straight line, all the merit of which is limited
to being straight; once the point of departure is determined,
it goes forward to strike an irresistible goal, the truth. But
all depends upon this point of departure, which considered
as principle, does not depend upon reason.[1] Reason is
indeed your domain, Lucifer, and you triumph there,

[1] See *Golden Verses of Pythagoras*, Fabre d'Olivet, p. 206.

provided you are allowed to lay down the principles. But if for your principles, which are those of instinct, one substituted those of intelligence, *adieu* to your triumph; it would vanish as vapour, and your reason itself would turn against you.

(36) Adah is vanquished; and see how she is recompensed by Lucifer. What frightful sublimity Lord Byron has put into the lines that follow! what a terrible picture!

> And the o'er-peopled Hell,
> Of which thy bosom is the germ!

(37) Lucifer himself acknowledges that he has aided the Eternal God in the work of creation; which admission has authorized me to draw several inductions, as has already been seen.[1]

(38) Oh! Oh! Lord Lucifer, how you do run on! Do you speak seriously? or does your poet add his belief to your inspirations? What! you say that your regions are everywhere, and that not only do you partake of those of the Most High, but even you possess a kingdom which does not belong to Him:

> So that I do divide
> *His;* and possess a kingdom which is not
> *His!*

But you do not think what you are saying. First, allow me to bring you back again to your good sense, if you have gone out of it; or let me beg your poet to put you in harmony with

[1] Act I, *Rem.* 9 and 16.

yourself. You have said, or he has made you say, that you were not from heaven:

ADAH

And you—
Are you of heaven?

LUCIFER

If I am not, inquire
The cause of this all-spreading happiness
(Which you proclaim) of the all-great and good
Maker of life and living things: it is
His secret, and he keeps it.

See therefore that, according to your confession, you are not from heaven. Let the motive of this exclusion be a secret; it is not the question here. The important thing is to know that you are excluded from all that which is celestial, and that, in consequence, your regions are far from being as extended as you pretend. Furthermore, not only do you not partake of the regions of the Most High, as your poet has made you say in a poetical enthusiasm, but even your own regions are His, as the force of truth will make you say when you shall be properly questioned.[1] What therefore do you possess, and in what place are you, in effect? Must Adam tell you simply, and will you hear him without disdain? "You possess all that is given you, and you are in all places whatsoever, in which you are necessary."

[1] Act II, *Rem.* 35.

REMARKS

PHILOSOPHICAL AND CRITICAL

ACT II

(1) This reflection, which is nonsense in the mouth of Cain after all that has passed, is only put there to bring out the diatribe which follows, in which Lucifer amuses himself with what religious and providential men understand by faith. He declares that he asks nothing from his followers; he is very right in acting thus, for they would accord him nothing. The master of spirits, interior or volitive, ought to know that men of his nature, who hold to the same principle as he, and who hold to this principle alone, have faith only in themselves; and that this faith, which they call confidence, strength of mind, or reason, is directed only according to the impulse of their will.

Lucifer does not ask, as condition for salvation, belief in him, but belief in oneself; for it is always true that one must believe in something. Now, the thing in which one believes is certainly that toward which one tends, or that in which one is; for it results from an irrefragable axiom of philosophy, that no being can act except where he is, or tend except where he tends, in the moment he so tends. Whether man, therefore, place his faith in God, in himself or in that force of things called destiny, he will act necessarily in one of the three principles that rule the universe; and will receive his strength from Providence, from volitive liberty or from fatidical necessity.

(2) Lord Byron has judged fitting to follow the modern astronomical system, and it must be said, he has drawn from it poetical tableaux of a great dimension. In giving justice once for all to the magnificence of his poetry, I shall abstain henceforth from speaking of it. My purpose in writing these *Remarks* has not been to discuss any system, either of astronomy, or of geology, or even of cosmogony. I have already declared that I wish to be occupied here only with moral principles.[1] I have translated, as closely as I have been able, the lines of the English poet; I have tried to make their beauties felt as much as the weakness of my talent has permitted. But in rendering his thoughts and his descriptions, I have not pretended to adopt them. These paintings can be true or false, in reality, without my being concerned in any manner. I have copied the design, I have imitated the colours, but as of a picture that had come from China or Japan, without troubling myself with its resemblance. If I should be transported into these countries, it would be possible for me, upon my return, to make descriptions that would not at all resemble those I had imitated.

(3) Here Cain speaks again without reflection, and only to bring about a new diatribe that the English poet wishes to have declaimed by Lucifer. This diatribe is, after all, only a commonplace, a thousand times repeated, upon the

[1] Act I, *Rem.* 1.

miseries of human life. The hidden intention of the declaimer is to make all the odium of these miseries fall upon the Creator of the world, in leaving it to be understood that they have entered into the plan of His work. His wish is thus to irritate the mind of Cain more and more, and bring it to an outburst which indeed happens according to his desires.

But this would not happen if the son of Adam wished to remember the instructions of his father. This father, whose character I have been obliged to enhance, since it is entirely sacrificed in the poem of Lord Byron, should have been able to hold, with his son, the discourse that I have given in the third *Remark* of the first Act. It results from this discourse, that at the moment when Adam, induced by Lucifer to lift his hand prematurely to the tree of knowledge, had plucked the fruit too soon, his life, too weak to resist the unexpected shock it experienced, was arrested in the course of the eternity it was destined to run, and took a retrograde movement. Adam, as he says, found himself exposed to the most horrible of sufferings, an eternal decline.

But the Creator of the world, who had foreseen the possibility of the accident, had prepared the remedy in power of being. Adam therefore left eternity, where he could no longer remain without undergoing an eternal agony, and entered into the course of time. The mode of his life was changed; and as he says, Cain was born with his brother to give birth to humanity. This humanity was therefore the result of an universal accident; and the beings which compose its actual universality, in whatever multitude of worlds one wishes to disseminate it, those who have composed or will compose it, suffer, have suffered or will suffer in an incalculable subdivision, and in an infinitely small proportion, the evils that Adam would have suffered *en masse*, and in one sole being, if he had not divided himself.

Thus the evils with which humanity finds itself unfortunately afflicted are the consequences of an accident, and entered not at all in principle into the plan of the Creator of the world, as Lucifer wishes to make it understood, in order to exonerate himself for having brought them about. These evils are not eternal since they are contained in limited time; they diminish progressively in intensity and in proportion as humanity extends itself in time and in space; and they will end by disappearing entirely, in being dissipated into what the geometricians call the infinitely small. In the same manner, to use a common comparison, a pound of salt, which would strongly salt a bucket of water, will salt a cistern very little, a pool scarcely any and a river not at all.

Space and time therefore, are the remedies for the evil Adam made for himself, throwing himself backward from eternity. This evil would have been eternal if Adam had conserved his universal life; he had to be divided in space to be cured, and to be divided to infinity by means of time. When this division is achieved, time will be arrested and, divisible space disappearing, Adam will return to his primitive state of indivisible and immortal unity.

I do not wish to stop at present to show up the injustice and impropriety of the murmurs that escape from certain fractions, infinitely small, of this great *all* called humanity, mankind, kingdom of man, Adam. They, considering themselves as isolated and without solidarity, believe themselves, in their extreme littleness, veritable Adams, and ask how the fault of the first Adam can be imputed to them. I think that there is not a single man who, having pursued the reading of my *Remarks* thus far, might not reply to them; moreover, I shall return to this subject.

(4) See the preceding *Remark*.

(5) Cain here returns to the idea already exposed in the first Act of the *Mystery*, the one that Lord Byron has taken care to put forward in his preface, to wit: that there is no allusion made in the Bible to a life to come, and that conse-quently Adam was ignorant of the existence of his soul and its immortality. I have already replied twice to this bold assertion.[1]

Now that I have explained, up to a certain point, the mystery of the origin of evil, I can add here, while always confining myself to the letter of the *Sepher* and without raising too much the veil that covers it, that it was precisely this immortality that made the greatest danger for Adam after his downfall. It exposed him, as I have said, to an eternal suffering. The Creator of the world wished indeed to spare him this suffering by keeping him away from the tree of Life, which would have perpetuated him in this fatal state. He did not tell him then that he was immortal; that was a thing too well known by Adam, and useless to say to him. A physician called to a sick person, does not inform him at first that he is a man, and that he was in good health before being sick; he indicates to him the remedy which should cure him. Now the sole means which could cure

[1] See the *Remarks upon Lord Byron's Preface*, and *Remark* 8, in the first Act.

Adam was his division in space, by means of time. God announced this division to him under the name of mutation, or *death*, but promised him that he would return to his first state.

(6) Lucifer openly declares the truth in saying that he is sorrowful, but he is careful not to say why he is so; I shall try to supply his silence when the occasion presents itself.

(7) This is not correct. Lucifer here shows signs of bad faith or ignorance. Man does not anticipate his immortality through suffering; he anticipates it, on the contrary, through limited time. If the master of spirits, the powerful, superb antagonist of the Eternal God, he who pretends to an immense knowledge,[1] had made the slightest usage of his power and his knowledge here, he would not have said such a stupid thing. But perhaps he has an ulterior motive; perhaps he wishes to make it understood that he does not believe the means employed for curing Adam of his malady can succeed. It seems, besides, that he has not, in this regard, very clear ideas. For, questioned by Cain upon the point as to whether torture is immortal, he replies in an evasive manner, and without saying either yes or no. He ought not to have hesitated, however, to be consistent; for if, through torture, man anticipates his immortality, it is evident that torture is eternal. Happily the one is no more true than the other. The contradiction into which Lucifer falls here is not the first that I have remarked upon, nor will it be the last.

(8) I restrain myself from speaking upon the ideas of the systems which fill this Act; but I cannot prevent myself

[1] Act I, *Rem.* 26, 27.

from stopping here to pay a just tribute of praise to the poetry of the author. This passage is full of the greatest beauty in the original.

(9) Cain, astonished at all that he sees, at the sight of the innumerable worlds with which space scintillates, cannot refrain from making a judicious reflection. In comparing these luminous worlds to the ephemeral flies that he has seen in the darkness, shining upon the greensward of the earth, he asks whether these diverse beings, so different in extent and in duration, are not equally guided by some intelligence. Lucifer, instead of replying directly and affirmatively to this question, which would have led Cain to make new reflections upon the Author of so many marvels, is content to propose to the son of Adam that he show him what these beings were formerly. Thus he backs out of the difficulty instead of resolving it; he dazzles Cain instead of enlightening him; and gives occasion for his poet to make, it is true, quite a number of beautiful lines. But after all it is reduced to describing phantoms pompously and reasoning upon illusions.

(10) Very good, Lucifer, you agree that life is more ancient than you. I accept your declaration in that which concerns you; as for what concerns the Being of beings, whom you regard as also less ancient than life, that is different. You are not competent to pronounce upon that which concerns Him, but only upon that which concerns you yourself. One can likewise believe you when you say that the greatest beings are mutable, except, naturally, the

One whom you have called the indissoluble, unique One.[1] Adam, relying upon this idea, soon proved to you that this mutability, to which you agree now and which you ought always to have known, was the cause of his downfall.[2]

This downfall, which you provoked in your own interest, but without foreseeing its fatal consequences, astonished you, as it astonishes you still; and the proof that you do not understand it, and that you have never understood it, even as Adam said to you, is that you assert space and time to be the only immutables:

> For *moments* only and the *space*
> Have been and must be all *unchangeable*.

This is absurd if you mean their appearance, all that strikes the senses of Cain, to whom you speak. But if you mean their principle or their essence in itself, that is very different. Cain does not know them; and you deceive him in speaking of one thing, while you let him understand another.

Listen to Adam, who is about to speak to you for a moment.

"No, *Nahash*," he says to you, "no. Space and time are not the only immutable things, since space, as you ought to know, is only a mode of immensity; and time, only a movement of eternity. If you can, fathom this profundity, and consider what I have already said: that after having been induced by you to pluck the fruit of knowledge, my life, at its dawn, which was advancing with a gentle and majestic course in eternity, stopped suddenly and took a retrograde movement. It then returned into the night whence it had

---

[1] Act I, *Rem.* 12.   [2] *Ibid.*, *Rem.* 16.

emerged and this was *space;* it then fell back in eternity, and this was *time.* Understand this, if you can, *Nahash,* and try to make it understood to your poet. He should make some very beautiful verses on it."

(11) This *Remark* has no other purpose than to stop the reader for a moment upon a pleasantry of Lucifer. After the politeness of the infernal spirits, of which Lord Byron has offered us several specimens, it is without doubt somewhat curious to know about their gaiety. I admit that I have weakened the witticism a little in my translation. Here it is in the original. When Cain asks whether, in the worlds that people space, there are also serpents, Lucifer replies:

Wouldst thou have men without them? must no reptiles
Breathe, save the erect ones?

(12) There is a contradiction here; for at one time Cain says that he does not seek to see death, and at another that he does seek to see it. The disturbance of his feelings, very natural in such a circumstance, can serve him as excuse; but nothing can excuse Lucifer for deceiving the son of Adam, in feigning to show him death, whereas he does not show it to him. The shadows of darkness are not death.

(13) Again a politeness from Lucifer. This is truly infernal.

(14) Now, Lucifer agrees that he has not shown death, but only its abode. That is different. He asks Cain if he

wishes to see death. This one, who sometimes says yes, sometimes no, decides not to; but he veils his pusillanimity by a violent diatribe both against God and against his father. They have made, he says, this gift that is so fatal to humanity; the one, in creating so cruel a destiny and the other in allowing himself to fall into it. He pities the fate of the innocent, condemned to lose life forever. . . . Lucifer tries unavailingly to interrupt, in showing him that he is cursing his father . . . he continues. A choir would be necessary here to stop this madman, whom a blind impious one is leading to crime. Let us try, in its place, to make Adam speak again.

"My son, my son," he cries to him, "where are thy thoughts wandering? What fatal frenzy agitates them! For a formidable word which strikes thine ears and which thou dost not comprehend, thou cursest the God who created thy father, and thy father who hath created thee! Stop, calm thyself; give thine intelligence time to clear thy reason. All the forces of thine instinct are aroused; thou art delivered to the impetuosity of thy passions; dost thou not feel it? Is thy heart mute in the midst of this tempest? Does it say naught in favour of thy father, in favour of thy God? If it is silent, at least let it listen. Oldest son of the first man, is this too much to ask of thee? Must thy father implore thee? Ah! if it be only to implore thee in order to snatch thee from the precipice that calls thee, Cain! hear me.

"Thou speakest ever of innocent ones condemned to death; and thine instinct, which suggests these words to thee, delivers them to thy reason, which accepts them without comprehending them. Lured thus into the vortex of the

most violent passions, it draws baleful consequences therefrom, by which it is more and more bewildered. But, my
dear Cain, this reason has been given thee to lead thee and
not to bewilder thee. Before allowing it to act thus, ask it if
it clearly comprehends the principles it poses. This one
moment of detention will suffice, if not to calm, at least to
prepare it for calm; for it will readily feel that it has admitted principles without discussing them, and only according to the words which represent them.

"Now words are not principles. In order that innocents
be condemned to death, it is necessary first that there be an
innocence and a condemnation: for the innocents can only
be such through innocence; and the condemned only through
condemnation. There must also be a death as the object of
this condemnation, and a death that this innocence can
undergo. Consider this well, my son; and conceive the
possibility that there be neither innocence, nor condemnation, nor death. What becomes of thy fit of passion then?
If only doubt be able to penetrate thy soul, and thy suspended reason no longer yield to the whirl of thine own will,
thou canst again know the truth. I am about to tell thee
how.

"Dost thou remember what I have repeated to thee
several times, pertaining to the fault I committed in taking
possession of the fruit of universal knowledge before my life
was far enough advanced to support its intoxication?[1] This
fruit, since we agree to give it this name, threw me into an
aberration which arrested the movement of my life, rendered
it retrograde instead of progressive as it should have been,

[1] Act I, *Rem.* 3.

and exposed me to the greatest danger to which an universal being can be exposed. I understood this danger; the Eternal God had clearly explained it to me. I could not exist except it existed, since the very principle that made it exist had furnished that of my existence; but I had all the means necessary to avoid it. *Nahash*, who held to the same principle, persuaded me to brave this danger; and my pride, in accord with him, made me believe that I should overcome it. He also believed; but we both deceived ourselves, for it was insurmountable. What I have gained over him through my guilty mistake is, that at least I have recognized it, whereas he still does not know it. He shows that he does not know it, in that, not having acted directly, he throws upon my inexperience, what is only the result of impossibility.

"Nevertheless, that my error could have taken place, and that my fault was possible, although its possibility was contained in the infinity of contrary possibilities, sufficed for the Eternal God, whose care embraces immensity, to have placed by the side of possible evil the irresistible means for its cure. This means, my son, was to change the mode of my existence; to put space into immensity, time into eternity, and what is still more admirable, to reduce unity to divisibility. This is what was done. Thus my suffering, which without that would have been unique and eternal, became temporal and fractional. From universal that I was I became particular; and the division which had to take place in my essence began. This division, which was manifested at thy birth and at that of Abel, is effectuated by generation. A great charm is attached thereto by the Eternal God, and it is without doubt one of His greatest benefits; for in order that this means of cure be able to operate, it is necessary that it be irresistible, as I have told thee.

"Now consider this. Thou, Cain, my first born, and thy brother Abel, you cannot say that you are innocent of my fault, since you are only myself conceived under other relations, and as a first division of my unity, which must be followed by a multitude of other divisions. To whatever extent these divisions may be carried in the future, whatever may be the number of my descendants, it will always be myself carried from unity into divisibility, and passed from immensity into space. These descendants will be only infinite fractions of an unique all, and each fraction, in reflecting me, will reflect my fault and will bear its part of the sorrow that this fault accumulated upon me. None of these fractions can say that it is innocent, since it will not be born in innocence; it cannot say that it is condemned, since it has not had condemnation, but only remedy applied to an evil in which this fraction participated with the all of which it is a part.

"And if this fraction, frightened as thou art now, of this death to which it is subjected, as all that which depends upon space and time is subjected, rebels against it, it will be proof of ignorance in more than one way. For all the means necessary will be given to it, according to the position in which it finds itself, for it to know death to be only a simple mutation, a change of condition leading from diversity to unity, in the same manner that birth leads from unity to diversity. It is even possible that this fraction of myself, if it purifies itself in the rays of intelligence, may attain to seize in my bosom all the truth that I possess, and may comprehend as well as I comprehend it, that to be born and to die are only the manifestation of this mysterious movement which bears immensity to space, and space to immensity, eternity to time, and time to eternity. Then for it, birth and death will be nothing more than a change of condition, a passing from the state of essence to that of nature, or from the state of nature to that of essence.

"I stop here, although I have still many things to add; but I fear to fatigue thine attention too much. Continue to follow *Nahash* into what he calls the abode of death; but remember that he shows thee only the phantoms of his imagination, figures in the vapours of his mind, where his dreams loom up and unceasingly mingle error with truth."

(15) The poet reverts perpetually to this idea, to which I have already replied several times.[1]

(16) A poor reflection, and founded upon the most vulgar and false opinion; it is largely refuted above.

(17) An exposition of a geological system mixed with truth and error, as is all that which Lucifer says. I have announced that my intention is not to occupy myself with it here.

(18) Continuation of the same system. I have already spoken of it in my book *l'Etat social de l'Homme*, in what pertains to universal politics.[2] I shall speak of it under other

---

[1] *Remarks upon Lord Byron's Preface*, Act I, *Rem.* 8.

[2] *Hermeneutic Interpretation of the Origin of the Social State of Man*, Fabre d'Olivet. Book V., ch. 8. Putnam.

relations, and in what pertains principally to cosmogony, in my work *La Théodoxie Universelle*, in which I shall comment upon Moses.

(19) Lucifer applies himself with marked attention to belittle, as much as he can, the actual universe, and to present the race of Adam from the worst side possible. He incessantly advocates the past at the expense of the present, and spreads over the future the lugubrious veil that is in his mind. I should like to attack him on this point of view of universal perfectibility, which he rejects violently; and I should have very great advantages over him. But to do so here it would be necessary to attack him in his systems of cosmogony and geology, and to enter into details that are foreign to this work and that would overstep greatly the limits that I have fixed. Perhaps I shall find another occasion. Moreover, if Lord Byron finds some satisfaction in seeing himself refuted in the manner in which I refute him, it will only depend upon him to enter the lists upon similar subjects. It will always be with pleasure that I measure myself with so distinguished an adversary.

(20) No, no, Lord Lucifer, this is not reality that you show. It is very far from it, I assure you. But when it is not a question of morals, it hardly matters what the magic lantern that one turns for children, shows. Continue to unroll your fantastic pictures; your poet describes them wonderfully.

(21) Cain, despite all the confidence he has in Lucifer, is not exactly of a mind to let him run down his world in-

cessantly; he is right. The worth of worlds, as that of men, does not consist, at least as I believe, so much in the mass of matter that composes them as in the force and purity of the intelligence that animates them. Now, that the mass of matter diminishes without cessation in the universe, and that, on the contrary, intelligence augments force and purity, is a necessary consequence of all that which Adam has told us in these *Remarks*. For if it is a spiritual malady that has determined the formation of this universe, as he gives it clearly to be understood, and if a curative means, applied to this malady, has constantly operated from the origin of things to bring about the cure, it is evident that matter, or the envelope of this means, must diminish unceasingly, in proportion as the spirit purifies itself in order to attain the height of perfection whence it fell.

(22) Again a satanic politeness. It is only put here to introduce the suffering of animals of which mention is made in the following article.

(23)　　　　　　"But animals—
　　　Did they too eat of it, that they must die?"

Lucifer skillfully puts this thought into the head of Cain to lead his imagination more and more astray, and prevent the effect of Adam's discourse which might have been recalled to his mind. He wishes to excite his indignation against the Creator of the world, by representing to him the suffering of animals as the height of injustice and barbarity on the part of this Creator; and he succeeds completely. This is great perfidy; for Lucifer ought not to be ignorant of what fatal causes have brought about the suffering of animals and their death. He ought to know well that there does not exist in respect to them, any more than in respect to men, either innocence or condemnation. Nevertheless, as the subject here is very arduous, I think it profitable to give the speech again to Adam, to explain this important point:

"My son," he says, "thou art disturbed concerning the fate of animals, as just now thou wert disturbed concerning that of men; I could not but commend this sentiment of generosity, if I could believe that it is pity alone which inspires thee. But I see, unfortunately, more irritation against the Creator of the world than real charity for his creatures. Nevertheless, that which thou takest here for an effect of his injustice and barbarity, is rather the greatest proof that he could give of his great mercy and goodness. This, I admit, is a little difficult to comprehend; but I do not despair of making it clear to thee, if thou wilt give me a little attention.

"When I was in my Eden, in the springtime of my immortal life, and in the calm of my innocence, I had received in principle from the Eternal God the creative faculty such as He Himself has, but only in the relation of my existence to His; for thou must not forget that I had been made in the image of the gods, and enjoyed all their prerogatives. I had received this faculty so that I might at pleasure embellish my abode with all the productions of elementary nature, and people it with all the creatures inferior to myself. Reflect, my son, once again upon this fact of universal creation, which thou hast never well understood; try to conceive that the Creator had made all these productions and all these creatures only in power of being, in germ, and that it appertained to me alone to make them pass into action, to develop them, to vary them infinitely and by the sole act of my will, to transport them in a moment from being to nothingness and from nothingness to being.

"I reigned as absolute master in my Eden, as all other celestial powers reigned in theirs. I could dispose of everything, produce everything, vary everything to infinity, without anything opposing my will. One single point was forbidden me: I could not take possession of the principle of my Eden, which belonged to the Creator, nor usurp the knowledge of this principle before the time fixed for this formidable knowledge to be given me. This knowledge contained in itself the knowledge of good and evil, even as it has been said. Thou knowest well enough how I was induced by *Nahash* to take possession of the principle. This being, whom thou callest Lucifer, and who hears me at this moment while I speak to thee, was persuaded and he persuaded me that, once possessor of this demiurgic force, I could act outside of my Eden as I acted within it, and rival the Eternal God in universal knowledge and in the employment of the two principles.

"I did that which he willed; but, as I have often enough related, the frightful effect which followed my criminal act was very far from responding to our expectation. The course that my life followed in eternity was arrested; everything around me stopped; and I saw, with an indescribable stupor, that the productions of my Eden and all the creatures I had put there, consolidated by a force which was unknown to me, depended no longer upon the action of my will. A retrograde movement had usurped all. It would be in vain for me to try to depict to thee my agony, as I was carried along with all the rest in this terrible movement. It is as far above thine imagination as all the united forces of all the men who shall exist forever are above the force of a single man.

"It was in the midst of this agony that the voice of the Most High caused itself to be heard by me, and His mercy deigned to lay down a limit, in changing, by His all-puissance, the mode of my existence. Nothing else could have changed it. Then I took forms analogous to those that my productions had taken. I became corporeal like them. The Eternal God could, without doubt, have annihilated my productions; but as the suffering, which was the inevitable consequence of my fault, could not be cured except by dividing itself to infinity, and as the more it was shared and divided, the more it became supportable and tended so much the quicker to be effaced, He deigned to make all the corporeal nature that was my work, co-operate in my cure. Thus the bulk of sorrows that must in the future weigh upon the totality of men born of me, was lightened in a very great degree by the division made with the animals.

"This was a great act of mercy on the Creator's part in favour of humanity; for, I repeat, the animals could have been annihilated; but considered as my work, they could not continue to live my life without partaking of its vicissitudes. They were not more innocent than my descendants are and shall be; for, once again I say it, all these beings, under whatever point of view one may consider them, are only I, only myself, whose unity is passed into diversity.

"Therefore, to wish that animals should experience no

fatigue, and should have no pain, would be to wish that men should endure the more, which would be neither just nor pious; for all have the same origin, with this difference alone: that that of man is more noble, and tends more directly to immortality.

"Now, after having enlightened thee on this important point, there is another upon which I wish to throw some light, although *Nahash*, who foresees my thought, seeks to arrest its flight. I shall say only a word in this respect, *Nahash*, and I shall even limit myself, if you do not provoke me by new acts. It is not alone the animals that partake of the sufferings of Adam, and lighten them in partaking of them, but this *Nahash* himself, this sovereign of spirits, as he entitles himself, Lucifer or Satan, as thou wouldst call him, partakes also of them, and lightens them in the same manner. He has not denied them, these sufferings[1]; but he has avoided telling their cause. He has even beclouded it as much as he could. There, I have told thee; think thereon; and may he himself think also, if he can."

(24) Lucifer talks here only for the sake of talking and to keep up the irritation in Cain's mind. Death is no more true in itself than birth is. The importance is in knowing the origin and the goal of each. So Adam has said.[2]

(25) Satanic pleasantry, which can be put on a level with the politenesses of Lucifer.

(26) Another pleasantry of the same nature.

[1] Act I, *Rem.* 8, 12, etc.; Act II, *Rem.* 6, 7, etc.
[2] Act II, *Rem.* 14.

(27) Lucifer strains to make it understood, in all this colloquy, that it was Eve alone who spoke to the serpent, not wishing to tell her husband or her children what the real object was that tempted her. This idea of the English poet is not new. One finds it expressed in a great number of rabbinical books, in much clearer terms than one sees here. It seems that Lord Byron, by a sort of gallantry which should please the fair sex, delights in throwing a very thick gloss over this passage of his poem. He has done well no doubt, but I believe that he would have done better still in avoiding this allusion altogether. As this idea of certain Karaite rabbis, or of certain visionary ascetics, is as false as ridiculous, I shall not dwell upon it.

(28) Cain is right; it was hardly worth the trouble of making him undertake so great a journey to teach him this, inasmuch as the discourse of Lucifer contains a very bitter irony upon the crime that he is driving Cain to commit, and that he foresees Cain will commit. Knowledge is assuredly neither in what this master of spirits has shown to the son of Adam nor in what he has told him. That it may occasionally be in what he has said, the reader is called upon to judge.

(29) That evil is necessary to most things in the actual state of things, is assuredly the most evident thing in the world; but that evil is necessary in itself, that it exists necessarily, and that it is in itself an absolute, independent being, is most assuredly false. Those who admit the two absolute principles of good and evil, can, in order to uphold their system, make as many reasonings as they wish; they

will never persuade a man who would or who could go for a moment beyond material limits.

Every man capable of interrogating his intelligence will see that he has a clear and distinct idea of the absolute good; whereas that of absolute evil can never enter his comprehension. What Lucifer says, a few lines after my *Remark*, fully confirms what I say, although this master of spirits affirms it in a contrary sense. For if all beings desire good, considered as good, and no one desires evil, considered as evil, it results from this notable difference in desire that good is the interior principle of every being, the leaven of life, as he says energetically; whereas evil is only an accidental effect in him, a sort of shadow, which indicates rather an absence than a reality.

Evil is in the universe as a malady is in an individual. One cannot say that the malady is an absolute state of this individual, his own and necessary condition; it is health on the contrary, that is or ought to be this state. Nothing is averse to health whereas everything is averse to malady. Thus, in the universe nothing is averse to good, all calls it to itself; and as to evil, all repulses it, nothing wishes for it. Good is therefore the primordial, absolute principle; whereas evil is only an accident brought about by a cause known or unknown. And by a means known or unknown, evil should be and will be taken away.

(30) It is useless to remark upon the cunning of this dialogue; the reader will feel the aim clearly. One single sentiment, love, was not yet disturbed in Cain; it was necessary to destroy it in his heart, as all the others had been destroyed, by showing the frailty of its cause. This infers

that Lucifer admits only a physical love and that he supposes no other in the son of Adam.

(31) Satanic politeness united with pleasantry of the same nature.

(32) This is the most trivial means that one could use to explain the presence of evil in the universe, the one that Bayle mocks the most and most justly. The English poet puts it in the mouth of Adam expressly to weaken more and more the character of the father of Cain and take away from him all his empire over his son. One has seen how Adam, come to himself again, has explained the origin of this formidable mystery, without entirely tearing aside the veil which should remain spread over it.

(33) The projects of Lucifer may be very great, in effect, but they are none the less vain. Adam has told him so already, in proper terms, and he is about to prove it in the next *Remark*.

(34) The choir of which I have already spoken would be more necessary than ever here, to temper the acrimony of Lucifer's discourse, and to cast at least some rays of light through the deceitful clouds with which he envelops Cain. The force that he displays to drive this unfortunate to crime, having no counter-weight, has truly an immoral effect; for, from the moment when the crime becomes irresistible and when the criminal is no longer free in his choice, the criminality disappears, and one sees in its place only a deplorable fatality. This dramatic fault, which the ancients knew how

to palliate by means of the choir, is to be seen, as I have said, in *Œdipus* and in *Phædra*. It is striking here. Let us try, in default of the choir we lack, to make Adam speak again. This time he addresses Lucifer; for his paternal sensibility does not permit him to address himself to Cain. He foresees too well what is about to happen.

"You conserve," he says to Lucifer, "the same sentiments that you had in the days of my lamentable adolescence; and, considering yourself still as a principle of the universe, you try to substitute yourself for another. Nothing has reformed you, *Nahash.* Neither my downfall nor yours has been able to enlighten you; mine, you regarded as the effect of weakness and foolishness; yours, as the work of hazard and the injustice of fortune. Your pride urges you to recover both; and while you meditate upon the most criminal action, an action most execrable in the eyes of a father, I should not be surprised if you believed you were rendering me a service, or if you should call magnanimity and strength of soul that which is only obstinacy and treachery.

"Your error is truly deplorable. Can I succeed in making you only just suspect it? I do not believe so. You repulse the light as fast as I show it to you; and in the profound darkness in which you are plunged, you oppose to the light of day I present you, the burning glare of a sulphurous firebrand. This firebrand, you say, enlightens you much better than mine, since it is yours, since it depends upon you, and since you apply it, as closely as you will, to the object you wish to see. That is true; but consider also that it spreads over objects a factitious light, which often lends

them colours not their own.   This light, limited in its extent,
never shines except where you are, and leaves all the rest in
shadow; so that it never shows anything but your thought
which you understand well, and to which you add faith.
This thought undoubtedly has force, but it is limited; and
when you oppose it to that of the Eternal God, as you have
done with me, as you are doing now with my son, it has
immensity against it; it is time struggling against eternity.

"You do not believe what I am saying to you, *Nahash*,
because, your greatest defect being lack of universality, you
lack universal prevision.   The prevision that you have is
restricted to contingent futures, and this prevision is short
when it is a question of eternity.   All your force is centered
because you make yourself centre, and you call weakness all
that which is not supported by the same motive that sup-
ports you.   You have made me wise, *Nahash*, at my own
cost and at yours.   At least try to profit by the knowledge
which, having precociously willed, we have paid for so
dearly.

"Let us reason coldly, if it be possible to reason thus at
the moment when you are making the most violent efforts to
deprive me of one son by the hand of the other.   What is
your design?   I hear you tell me what you will not fail to tell
Cain, if he asks you the same question: to reign. [1]   You wish
to reign, I know it.   You also wished to reign when you
inspired me, scarcely entered into life, to take possession of
what could only be life's complement,—universal knowledge.
By favour of this knowledge, you hope to seize, in its in-
accessible sanctuary, the secret principle of life; and flatter-

[1] Act II, *Rem.* 37.

ing yourself that you possess one of the two principles of the universe, which in reality is very uncertain, you doubt not that you will attain to the possession of both, and dominate, by their means, the absolute Being who dominates you.

"But remember the fatal catastrophe which was the sequel of my attempt. It should be present in your mind, and there is no need, I think, to depict it to you in the same manner as I have depicted it several times to Cain.[1] You know well enough how the mode of my existence was changed; how I passed from immensity into space, from eternity into time, and from unity into diversity. You passed with me, and you were obliged, on your side, to share the bulk of sorrow that must be shared by all corporeal nature on its side, so that the burden, thus divided, weigh less upon this immense division of myself called mankind. This was just, since you had shared my fault, in a proportion at least equal to mine, and since, if the results had been happy, as you expected, you would have usurped the greater part.

"Nevertheless, you did not submit to this act of justice, as all corporeal nature submitted, and so hasten, by your submission, the moment of my reinstatement in my primordial existence,—a reinstatement that would necessarily have brought yours about. On the contrary, you rebelled. Your pride persuaded you that you ought not to submit to chastisement for a fault which concerned me alone; for you saw in my fault, not what it really was, the consequence of an attempted impossibility, but that of an incapacity which failed. You continued to consider your design of usurpation as the thought of a powerful and magnanimous

[1] Act I, *Rem.* 3; Act II, *Rem.* 14.

mind, the triumph of which the Eternal God had avoided only through the weakness of the instrument employed. You persisted therefore in your movement of opposition. Considering what would suit you best to do in the position in which you were, you judged that it was to take possession of me again, no longer in my unity, since that had become impossible by my breaking, but in my diversity. You thought to reconstruct from all my fractions, the conquest of which you thought would be easy, a new unity which would be absolutely given up to you, and with which you might recommence your struggle with the Eternal.

"You understand what I say, *Nahash*, and you see clearly that I read your thought as easily as you pretend to read Cain's. But here is something that has happened, which you did not foresee; for, even as I have just said, it is not in prevision that the force of your genius shines. You awaited the divisions of my unity, as they appeared in diversity, and you hoped to seize them all readily and fill them with your thought. However, after having considered the first two which have appeared, you have seen with astonishment that they were not of the same nature and that two powers very different were manifested in them.

" This suddenly made you comprehend, because of the faculty you have of binding contingent futures, that my divisions, innumerable in posterity, might indeed be divided into two classes; and might obey, in the movement of their souls, two powers opposed to each other but not absolutely contrary. Cain appeared to you to be the type of the first of these classes, and Abel that of the second. You examined their characters; and without recognizing in full the powers upon which they depend, you clearly felt that it was impossible to dominate them equally. This discovery, which disconcerted your projects, should have stopped you; but no, your stubbornness has been only stronger, and your pride, irritated by it, has suggested to you the most odious means to attain your ends.

"Is it necessary to say what you have designed? You have designed to stifle in its cradle a half of myself, that is to say, that class of my descendants of which Abel should be the head and type. Your purpose is that the providential power which dominates in it should be extinguished in its origin; and the other class of my descendants, whose type is in Cain, dominated by the power of the will of man, should remain alone in the universe. It then would be subservient to you by the very crime that you inspired in its chief.

"These are your projects, *Nahash;* I have just named the two powers that you have before you: on the one side divine Providence, personified in my son Abel, and on the other, the will of man, personified in my son Cain. You want the will of man to annihilate Providence. In universal principle, this is impossible without doubt, but it can be in the particular forms of the world. I even foresee that it will be, and that you will succeed to a certain point.

"Can I presume to stop you, while the crime is still not committed? One single means presents itself to me for this. Here it is: *Nahash*, it is not to your interest to commit this crime; it will not give you what you expect. The difficulty that you pretend to destroy will only be put off, and putting it off will augment its force. If Abel falls under the blow of his brother, you will have done what you judge proper, but not what you wish; for the results of this crime will be precisely what you do not wish."

(35) Observe how Lucifer says here that the unknown places inhabited by the Eternal are everywhere. Consequently he was wrong in saying that he possessed an empire extended beyond the domain of the Eternal.[1]

(36) The wish Cain makes is very beautiful and nobly expressed; but as it bears upon the supposition of the existence of the two principles, independent one of the other, it cannot be effectuated in the manner in which he understands it; at least not according to the Mosaic doctrine, upon which the poem of Lord Byron is founded.

(37) Here therefore is the purpose of the crime Lucifer meditates: he wishes to reign. But before thinking of using a means so culpable, has he at all examined the possibility of the result? Has he shown by any reasoning, even specious, that he has any chance favourable for himself in the combat that he aspires to open with the Eternal? No. One sees plainly that it is his pride alone, his indomitable will, which precipitates him into this combat. Even the hope of gaining the victory is not based upon any striking illusion. He fights with a blind fury, and the weapons he uses are those of weakness and of perfidy. Thus here then is Lucifer, of his own confession, ignorant and cowardly. Cain himself is struck by this frightful consequence. He cannot prevent himself from reproaching Lucifer for doing evil.

[1] Act I, *Rem.* 38.

This is the only time that Lord Byron makes the hero of his drama reason justly. This reasoning could lead the author far, and show him that in supposing two principles in the universe, the one good, the other evil, and as he appears to believe, equal in power, and both independent, the one he calls Lucifer is really the principle of evil, as Cain charges. One would say that, terrified himself with this consequence, which he draws despite himself, he has averted his eyes, and hastened to pass on.

(38) Cain stops Lucifer here to say a very judicious thing to him. If, indeed, this master of spirits is alien to the works of the Creator of the world, as he says, let him then leave its creatures in peace. But Lucifer contradicts himself here in an obvious manner, for he has said elsewhere that he aided the Creator of the world in his work.[1] Adam, in taking up this confession, has already shown Lucifer that not only is he not alien to the work of creation, but he is even eminently necessary there. The evil he has made can be compared to one that a master mason might make. This one, believing himself misplaced, having vainly tried to put himself in the place of the architect, and not having succeeded, might maliciously cause the half raised edifice to collapse. But if it collapsed in such a manner that he should be entangled in its débris, he would be seized, chained by the feet and forced as a convict to mend at his own cost all that he had spoiled.

(39) It is quite natural that Lucifer, in the state in which I have just depicted the master mason, seeks to find assist-

[1] Act I, *Rem.* 13, 33, 37.

ants; but what is not very politic on his part is making it understood as crudely as he does here to those whom he tries to fasten to the same chain that holds him.

(40) Cain obviously puts himself, by the force of his soul, above Lucifer. If he remained at this height, and nothing prevented him from it, the master of spirits could do nothing with him.

(41) Lord Byron has visibly attached much importance to these lines, which depict the miserable situation into which Lucifer is about to plunge Cain, after having filled his head with so many brilliant illusions:

> And now I will convey thee to thy world,
> Where thou shalt multiply the race of Adam,
> Eat, drink, toil, tremble, laugh, weep, sleep and die.

The bitter irony they contain strikes Cain, who cries justly:

> And to what end have I beheld these things
> Which thou hast shown me ? . . .

Lord Byron has summed up in these words, the criticism of his poem. What he adds is only to lead up to the superb diatribe which he puts into the mouth of Lucifer.

(42) Very beautiful, Lord Lucifer, very beautiful! What you repeat here with so much emphasis, Adam demonstrated as false when you said it for the first time.[1] It is not true that you possessed all the things you say; neither is it

---

[1] Act I, *Rem.* 33, 34, 38.

true that you have battled, or that you still would battle.
All, for you, is limited to this: pretending to be what you are
not; pretending to have done what you could not have done.
After all, justice must be rendered to your poet; he enters
admirably into your spirit, and makes you speak with a
sublimity that has something terrifying in it.

(43) This is very true; and, like all that is in this passage,
extremely eloquent in the original. But who does not feel
that it is only a displacement of ideas, and that the English
poet transports to one principle that which belongs to the
other? Lucifer speaks here as principle of good, and states
as fact that which is in question. First of all, do there exist
two principles? And, in the case that these two principles
exist, which would one take for that of good? Would it be
Lucifer, who poses as such?

But it results from the discourses of Adam, the proofs of
which are unimpeachable in the Mosaic doctrine followed by
Lord Byron, that there is but one sole principle of all things,
from which all emanates, and which acts in the universe
under three modifications. These modifications may be
considered as three distinct principles, as is sometimes done
for the facility and clarity of the reasoning. That which is
presented here under the name of Lucifer, named *Nahash* by
Moses, is not even one of these three primordial modifications. It is only a sort of dispensation of one of these
three modifications or secondary principles. This dispensation, which can be conceived of as a leaven, an interior
motive, is neither good nor bad in itself; it is indifferent, in its
source, to good as to evil, and only becomes one or the other

by the use the will makes of it. Therefore the principle of evil, properly so-called, does not exist.

Evil, as I have repeated often enough in these *Remarks*, is not a principle, that is to say, a thing existing by itself; it is an accident. It is that leaven of which I have spoken, exalted and put into a sort of disordered and inharmonious fermentation, which, instead of cherishing life, corrupts and destroys it. Thus, acting outside its primitive properties, this exalted leaven can be styled the genius of evil, because of its disastrous effects. But as it has nothing principiant in it that cannot be recovered in proportion as it is used, or be reformed in proportion as it is divided, it ensues that it tends unceasingly to be checked, and that in effect it is checked.

Good alone is an absolute principle. This is proved, as I have already shown, in that man has a distinct idea of it, whereas he has none of absolute evil. Any man can desire good for good in itself and considered as good; but no man would desire evil for evil in itself, and considered as evil. Good is the root of every idea, even of that of evil; but not only is evil not the root of every idea, but it is not even the root of its own idea; consequently evil is not an absolute principle.

Without doubt it has depended upon Lord Byron alone to give momentarily to his Lucifer the attitude and the language of the principle of good. But, according to the rôle he has made him play, the impious declamations that he has put into his mouth, the execrable action toward which this spirit is visibly driving Cain, this is a confusion of ideas, a violation of principles too evident to pass in silence.

> La poésie a ses licences, mai
> Celle-ci passe un peu les bornes que j'y mets.

REMARKS

PHILOSOPHICAL AND CRITICAL

ACT III

(1) This scene between Cain and Adah is very beautiful. It bespeaks in its author, beside the talent for poetry that none can dispute him, a great understanding of the human heart, and much habit of the theatre. The gradation of sentiments is perfectly observed; the passions of Cain are well developed; all shows the terrible situation of his soul. This scene, and in general all this third Act, would give great effect in presentation. But in order that the first two Acts might be presented, and that the profound colour of impiety which rules throughout the totality of this drama might be lightened, it would be necessary to have an aerial choir to represent the principle of good, and to give the character of Adam some of the force that the poet should not have entirely effaced.

But, as my intention has not been to dwell upon the dramatic art in itself, I shall not stop upon the praise that might be given to several passages of this Act, remarkable chiefly from this side. I shall only continue my moral exploration. I have said nothing of the cosmological and geological systems which fill the second Act; I am likewise silent concerning the theatrical situations which abound in the third. This resolution will render my *Remarks* less frequent in this Act than in the other two; for, as it is only a development of that which precedes, one will see that I have nearly always said in advance all that might be said.

The ideas upon which this first *Remark* bears are not new; I have already refuted them.[1] Enoch, the son of Cain, is not innocent of the fault of Adam, for the reasons I have shown. All the plaints of Cain are only declamations to which the poetry of Lord Byron lends more or less force or charm.

(2) Cain deceives himself. If he remembered what Adam said to him, he would know that, as all the descendants of this universal man endure fractionally a part of the sorrow that he has incurred, all will equally enjoy his primitive felicity at the time of his reinstatement; for this absolute reinstatement can take place only when the last and least of his fractions shall be completely purified.

(3) Cain ever forgets what his father has said several times to him: that if he had not been subject to death, he would not have been born. Death in the physical life is only a pure and simple consequence of birth. It is not death that should astonish in this life, it is birth. This first step is indeed more mysterious and more inexplicable than the last.

(4) This is not exact. Man cannot say without lying to himself that he is nothing; and still less that God has created him to be nothing. God has created him, on the contrary,

[1] Act II, *Rem.* 14.

to become one of the greatest celestial powers. An accident is opposed to his development; but this retrograde movement in eternity, which is called *time*, will not prevent him from attaining to his fair destinies, when the perfection, from which he has turned aside, shall be attained anew by means of perfectibility.

(5) Now Cain recommences to curse his father, and always for the same reasons. These reasons, as I have shown, are without foundation; but after all, if they had foundation, of what avail so impious a fit of passion? The fate of Cain, or that of his son, are they changed? Not at all. I recall that at the beginning of this drama, Abel made this same reflection to his brother, but in accompanying it with another, which in the situation of things, could only augment the irritation of Cain. Here are his words:

> Why wilt thou wear this gloom upon thy brow,
> Which can avail thee nothing, save to rouse
> The Eternal anger?

That murmuring serves to no purpose, that it even harms the one who utters it, is something a volitive man of the character of Cain can arrive at comprehending; but that this murmuring rouses the Eternal anger, as Lord Byron makes Abel say, is something such a man will never comprehend. The more he is led to admit the existence of the Most High, and to surround this existence with all the faculties and all the perfections that his idea must necessarily involve, the less he will admit that this existence could be troubled by anger. For as, by himself and despite his fit of passion, he well judges that anger is an imperfection, he will be careful not to place it where only absolute perfection can exist. He will therefore have a very bad idea of the judgment of a person who holds such converse with him; and if he cannot, as in the situation of Cain, regard the person who speaks with the scorn that one must give to imposture or stupidity, at least he will consider him with the disdain that weakness of mind or falseness of judgment inspires. This is how, in wishing to prove too much, one proves nothing. Let us make here a comparison.

A fatal accident has reduced your house to ashes, and also that of your neighbour, who, by his negligence or awkwardness, has let the fire reach his. Do you give yourself over to imprecations against the fire that has devoured your home? Do you curse the unfortunate neighbour, victim like yourself of imprudence? Do you accuse heaven? Do you accuse the earth of your disaster? Yes, you reply to me, that is in human nature. No, I avow, it is not there; it is you who put it there, by voluntary neglect of your intellectual faculties. It is not in human nature to augment its evil expressly, and without any hope of good; and do you do anything else by your imprecations? Does a passerby who hits his foot against a stone, strike the stone anew with his foot to increase the pain that he already feels? Often, you tell me. Then he is an idiot who behaves like a brute beast. A man purely instinctive is satisfied with grazing his foot, and passes on; a passionate man cries out that he is hurt, and asks what the stone is doing there? Why has not some one taken it away? An intellectual man reflects that this stone is badly placed, that it might bruise another, and puts it aside.

But let us return to our first comparison. If while your house is burning, and as you express thoughtless imprecations someone comes to you calmly, saying that your imprecations serve only to irritate the intensity of the fire and precipitate conflagration, you enter into an even greater fury; for you add to the irritation that your misfortune causes you, the indignation that you receive from a false reasoning. But if, with all the warmth of interest, someone shows you that your fits of passion are of no avail against the accident that has befallen you; that you are only losing precious time; that you are harming yourself by paralysing your strength; and that it is worth more in such a circumstance to think of repairing the evil than to be troubled by the fatality which caused it; then, restored to reason by reason itself, you try to arrest the progress of the fire if there is yet time; and if it is too late, you begin to help your neighbour to raise his home, so that afterward he may help you to raise yours.

Cain ought to maintain an analogous conduct; and without returning incessantly to the past, think more sensibly of the future. Neither the weak Abel nor the sensible Adah can pretend to enlighten him. He will break the thought of the one, and force the thought of the other to sympathize with his. Adam is the only one who might take the speech here. He will take it.

(6) Always the same idea presented under diverse aspects; always the innocence of Adam's descendants put in evidence to accuse the Creator of the world of injustice and barbarity. But let the volitive men, who think as Cain does in this respect, prove their premises but once. Let them

cease to declaim, and let them reason. I have proved that this innocence does not exist, and that where there is no innocence, there are no innocents. Let one overthrow my proofs, if he can; and then let him establish contrary ones if he can.

(7) Adam has replied to all this, principally in his last two discourses.[1] As to the knowledge that Cain asserts can only be acquired by an inconceivable crime, it has, in effect, already been acquired; but only by Adam, whom it has overwhelmed, and who could transmit it to his posterity only in a multitude of fragments, because it was broken as he, and because it passed with him from unity into diversity at the time of his change of existence. This is why men, even the wisest, possess knowledge only in small parts, and why they have so much trouble in uniting their divergent opinions when they wish to reconstruct the fallen edifice in its primitive unity.

(8) The English poet makes Cain repeat words which he has heard spoken in a figurative sense, and which he does not comprehend. He is pleased to put anew into the mouth of Adam's son extravagant discourses such as he has heard held by certain energumens, either in the taverns of London or elsewhere. And he ends by raising the feelings of this madman to such a point that through pity he is about to outrage nature in what is most inviolable and prelude the murder of his brother by that of his son. It is at this moment, when the unhappy Adah casts herself down before him, that Adam should again address him.

[1] Act II, *Rem.* 23 and 34.

"Miserable one," he would say to him, "where does thy blind fury bear thee and what dost thou think of doing? Thou believest, by dashing thy son upon this rock, to be able to shield him from the destiny that awaits him, whatever this destiny may be. Thus thy proud weakness would struggle against the All-Powerful, and thine impotency arm itself against the universal force! Insensate! hast thou not heard me repeat a thousand times that this Creator, God, whose justice thine ignorance accuses, is absolute master both of death and of life, and that He alone can dispose of them? Even if thine inconceivable blindness should lead thee to deprive thy son of life, or even to destroy his life with thine own hands, thinkest thou that thou couldst annihilate the one or the other? Thy will can, at the most, destroy forms momentarily and suspend their functioning; but to take them away from the laws which rule the universe! that is impossible for thee.

"These laws, to which I am subjected as thou art, will that I divide myself, will that space be filled with my productions; and thou wouldst pretend to oppose thyself to them! Eldest son of the first man, fulfill thy destiny. Wert thou beyond all the worlds, the luminous orbs which *Nahash* has shown thee, thou wouldst still be under the eye of the Eternal; and His all-powerful hand would, if He deemed it proper, force thee to come and retake the place thou hadst deserted.

"Reflect, Cain, upon what I have just told thee, while there is still time, and while this *Nahash*, who inspires thee, learns from my mouth that to recoil from difficulties is not to conquer them; nor is to change forms to annihilate them."

(9)   What may this mean?

That is to say whence comes Cain's terrible trouble? Abel, who asks, ought to know. But one sees that he is utterly ignorant of it. The excessive confidence of this providential man astonishes as much as it afflicts. The English poet has expressly thickened the veil over the eyes of Abel, so as to render more striking the rigour and injustice of the fate that menaces him. He wishes that his death be imputed to the Creator of the world, Who offers no obstacle to it, Who seems, on the contrary, to behold with indifference the downfall of his adorer. On one side Cain is seen, driven to murder by an irresistible force which masters him without his knowledge; without wishing it, without foreseeing it, he is about to commit the most horrible outrage. Abel, on the other side, is calm and cold; he experiences none of those presentiments which ought to have enlightened him upon the danger he runs.

The intention of the poet here is evident. He wishes to show by a reputed sacred fact, which he gives as historic, that Providence takes no part in any of the affairs of this world, or that, if it does take part, it is powerless to prevent evil. He wishes the reader to infer, as much in respect to what happened in Eden as to what is actually happening outside, that the being whom he calls Lucifer, and whom we believe to be the genius of evil, the devil, is the sole active principle and the sole powerful principle; since it is he alone who acts and who acts efficiently in his will. This plan, which Lord Byron scarcely dissimulates, is conducted with much art, and it is not without some trouble and some reflection that one can discover its vice.

It has been seen how, in the letter I wrote to the author, I took away the ground upon which he stood, which reduced all his conclusions to nothingness. But as he could claim this ground by denying even the very examinations of my proofs and by considering himself as sufficiently enlightened by the English translation of the *Sepher* of Moses, I have condescended to this pretension, so as to leave him no refuge against the truth that I would make him hear; and I have consented to fight him even upon a ground the reality of which I do not admit. It has been seen, if one has followed with any attention the sequence of these *Remarks*, that all which came to pass in Eden has been explained, even in the literal sense, without leaving any sort of prize to the noble poet; and that the all-puissance of the Creator, His justice and His mercy have been put above every attack.

It would be useless, I am certain, to prove here in the same manner the permanent action of His Providence in the care of the things of this world. This undertaking, although possible, could not be effectuated in a frame so limited as that in which Lord Byron is contained. An action so lofty, so irresistible, so universal as that of Providence, can only be appreciated in particular facts with the greatest difficulty; and this is why: the power of the will, which the Eternal has made to be one of the regulating principles of the world, being essentially free, cannot and should never be forced in anything, unless the force that constrains it comes from itself.

Now, if Providence acted directly and ostensibly in the things of the world, its irresistible action would leave no place for the acts of the will. There would be no longer any liberty, since all that there would be to do would be done in advance in the thought of Providence, which is immutable; and if there were no liberty, there would be no morality, and vice and virtue would become indifferent. It is in this accord of providential action, necessitated by divine pre-science, and volitive action, free in its essence, that the All-Powerful shines forth. The man who complains of not comprehending the mystery of this accord, complains of not being all-powerful; for if he could comprehend it, he would be able to arrest it, because, his will being essentially free, its movements are irresistible; and if he could arrest it, he would be equal to the All-Powerful, which is absurd to think.

I have endeavoured, in a work of great length, to make understood the action of Providence in the things of this world[1]; I have followed, as much as my strength permitted, the traces of this divine power during the long interval of twelve thousand years; and I have called attention to those events in which it is the most clearly manifested. I refer the reader who would sound the depths of a matter so impor-tant, to this work. I can here give only the simple indications.

Supposing that the event related by the English poet were historical, purely and simply, and that it did not pertain to the highest mysteries of cosmogony, this is what I could say of it: it is the power of the will alone which determines events, and which, acting in the essence of its liberty, brings them about irresistibly. Providence can do

---

[1] *Hermeneutic Interpretation of the Origin of the Social State of Man*, Fabre d'Olivet. Putnam.

nothing at all as to their forms; only, since it has provided them with power of being, and since all the possibilities are constantly present before it, it has prepared also the infallible means of foreseeing all the consequences. I shall tell, in the proper place, what this means is.

Concerning the form the poet has given to this event, considered as natural, I say that this form is utterly outside nature. Never can a personage of importance such as Abel is here, die a violent death, except the blow which menaces him be known to him in advance, by the effect of a presentiment more or less clear. It is this very presentiment that serves as a sort of physical proof of the existence of the soul, and gives proof to those who have need of it.

One has only to glance, even superficially, through history, and he will see that all the personages of note who were to be assassinated have known it. If all have not evaded death, it is that their will has not been strong enough for that. This weakness of will was chiefly remarkable in Cæsar, in Henry IV., in the duc de Guise, in the Duke of Buckingham, and in a host of others that it is useless to name. It seems to me that a man like Lord Byron ought to have known this. Perhaps he thought to make the downfall of Abel more theatrical by making it wholly unexpected to him; but he is mistaken. As to the odium he pretends to make rebound against Providence, all that which precedes ought to demonstrate its falsity.

(10) This obstinacy of Abel, which is incited by nothing, is bad and out of place here under whatever point of view it is considered. If the noble poet has thought, by this observa-

tion, to accuse Providence more and more of indifference, he has only given to be understood that he had never reflected upon the manner of this power's activity.

(11) This prayer of Abel is expressly turned so as to put in evidence the weakness of the character Lord Byron has given him. In exaggerating several consequences, the poet has sought to throw disfavour upon the principles which are here contained; but these principles remain none the less, although the consequences are badly drawn. After all, it was not in such a prayer that Lord Byron could give flight to his talent; and he has not done so.

(12) Here is where the poet displays all the resources of his eloquence; here is where he opposes the character of the providential man to that of the volitive man. These two characters are perfectly depicted; the first, in these lines which Abel speaks:

> Sole Lord of Light!—
> Without whom all were evil, and with whom
> Nothing can err, except to some good end
> Of thine omnipotent benevolence—
> Inscrutable, but still to be fulfill'd.—

the second, in these lines which Cain declaims:

> As thou wilt! since all
> Rests upon thee; and good and evil seem
> To have no power themselves, save in thy will;

These two prayers, opposed with art, expose the system of the English poet, and distinctly show the purpose of his poem. I have spoken enough of this purpose for it to be known; and to refer one by one to the consequences that follow would only mean to say again all that I have said, both in my preliminaries and in my *Remarks*. This would assuredly be an idle repetition; for the reader knows all that I might still say, if he has wished to know it.

(13) The sacrifice of Cain is rejected, not because it is badly dressed, but because it is presented in an improper manner. It is this which the two brothers do not appear to feel, especially Cain, who is filled with wonder at the avidity with which the fire from heaven fastens upon the blood and devours the flesh of the victims. In Cain's state of mind, he is not in condition to attend to a religious duty, and Abel ought to have seen it.

The volitive man, as long as he persists in his own will, and does not submit it to the universal will, ought not to approach the altar in office of pontiff. His place is in the camp; the sword is better in his hands than the censor. The providential man, so long as he remains purely providential, is equally misplaced under arms. The perfection of man would consist in the union of the two characters, the providential and the volitive. But this is extremely difficult, almost impossible, without the mediatory action of a third character, which, at the time in which our poet has placed the terrible scene we are examining, was not yet born. The birth of this third character was really brought about by the disastrous event which followed this scene, as I shall tell presently.

(14) The English poet has wished to show that the first
quarrel raised among men was a religious quarrel, and that
the first victim death struck stained the altar with blood.
This appears true; but notice, I pray you, that the fanatic
who strikes, and who sheds the blood, is not the providential
and religious man.   It is, on the contrary, the volitive man,
opposed to religion, who commits the first crime.   Consider
also that it is not religion in itself which is the cause of the
quarrel, it is the form of worship which is the pretext. Cain
does not find it objectionable that his brother is devoted to
religion.   He consents even to follow it himself in a certain
manner.   But he does not wish to be constrained by such
and such a rite, such and such a ceremony; and when he has
made his prayer, which he finds good for himself, and when
he has offered a sacrifice that he judges even purer than that
of his brother, his irritation is at its height when it is said
to him that his prayer is impious and that his sacrifice is an
abomination.   His pride revolts; all his passions are aroused;
he believes himself persecuted and becomes persecutor.

If one will give attention to the causes which, in all times,
have provoked the wars called religious, one will see that
always they have had their source in the forms of worship,
especially in the politics that later on take possession of these
forms, and that religion in itself never counts for anything.

What takes place here between Cain and Abel is not
religious, as the noble poet would have it believed.   These
are two opposed characters, which are destined to unite in the
course of nature, but which clash unseasonably and are
broken; both are equally great and good, equally in their
place.   It would have been necessary to let them develop in

silence, to produce, by their union, the perfection of human nature; but passion, exalted and already prevaricating, which Lord Byron calls Lucifer, is opposed to this union, and determines, by the destruction of one of them, another series of events, even as Adam has just informed us.

(15) The remorse Cain expresses, with admirable energy, proves that he has no criminality in him, and that the crime he has committed is the effect of an irresistible fatality. This fatality falls back wholly upon Lucifer, who is its author. Providence, as I have already shown, could not arrest this event, as it might have done, without itself violating its own laws; for although it is all-powerful, its all-power is not exercised in the manner in which certain thoughtless men believe. It cannot act in such a way that liberty be not free, and necessity be not forced; but it can act so that liberty and necessity arrive at the same goal by different roads, and end by being identical. This is what it does.

I am not stopping to remark upon the poetical beauties which shine here in detail. I have said that this would not be my task, and besides I should have too much to do. However I cannot refrain from noting as sublime the passage where I have placed my remark:

What's he who speaks of God?

If Lord Byron has felt, in all its extent, the sublimity of this interrogation, as I certainly like to believe, he must see a new proof of the truth that he has sought to combat and that I have forcibly established: that the principle of good is the sole principle of the universe, and that evil, in whatever manner it is presented, is only a transient accident wholly deprived of basis.

(16)   Father!—Eve!—
      Adah!—Come hither! Death is in the world!

Here again is a sublimity which it is impossible for me to pass in silence. "Death is in the world!" There was no like situation which could have inspired an exclamation so new, so strong, which could have shaken the soul so profoundly, and which might have borne so many ideas at once.

(17) I beg the reader to notice here the development of the characters Lord Byron has given to Adam and Eve, so that he may judge if what I have said of them in my letter to the noble poet, and in the course of my *Remarks*, is not exact.

(18) What frightful imprecations! I dare not stop myself here, for fear of saying things unfitting, which would lead away from my subject. What a spouse! what a mother Lord Byron has presented to us in the first wife and mother! Cain is a volitive man; but his character has at least magnanimity and grandeur. Eve is also a volitive woman. But, great God! from where has the poet drawn his model?

(19) Adam, instead of arresting the course of maledictions that a disordered passion dictates to his wife, leaves her tranquilly to go on to the end, being contented no doubt with having said to her before:

> Eve! let not this
> Thy natural grief, lead to impiety!

But Eve, who knows very well how to impose silence upon him when anything disagreeable touches her, says to him:

> Oh! speak not of it now: the serpent's fangs
> Are in my heart.

Eve is not at all of a mind to respect the deplorable excess of Adam's sorrow; she stops only when, undoubtedly, her rage lacks expression or her breast breath; and her kind spouse, who has let her say all she wished, confirms her sentence in ordering Cain to depart. That in effect Cain could not dwell longer near his father, after the crime he has just committed, is certain; but at least Adam owes him some instructions. One would say that Lord Byron has felt all this by putting into the mouth of Adah these two lines full of sentiment:

> Oh! part not with him thus, my father: do not
> Add thy deep curse to Eve's upon his head!

(20) Adam replies:

> I curse him not: his spirit be his curse.

This is better, but it is not enough; Adam should speak here for the last time.

"All my efforts have been in vain," he would say, "I have been unable to avert a fatal evil. Miserable Cain, what crime hast thou committed; or rather what crime hast thou permitted thy hand to commit! Cruel instrument of a spirit still more cruel, how hast thou not seen the abyss into which he has driven thee? But, guilty before thee, have I the right to curse thee? No; thy mother, by doing it, in a fit of passion which I censure, has gone beyond her rights, has usurped those of Heaven. It belongs to the Eternal God alone to pronounce upon thy fate. The duty of a father, far from anticipating His justice, is rather to call upon His mercy; I implore it for thee. May His clemency again equal and even surpass that of which I was the object! His goodness, which enlightens me, says that this will be so.

"In the meantime hear, before we separate forever, what will be the effect of thy crime in the future.

"This haughty spirit, who has taken thee about so much in space, and who has borne into thine imagination the gigantic ideas that are in his, ever mixing truth and error, *Nahash* has succeeded in his designs. But far from arriving at the goal where he aspired to attain by this success, he has, on the contrary, put himself far from it, by lengthening the time of my reinstatement and by augmenting the obstacles that oppose it, without at all being able to prevent its accomplishment.

"This reinstatement which, as I remember having told thee, consists in the return of the diversity to the unity, might have been effectuated by means of my first two divisions, thee and thy brother Abel. In you were manifested two universal powers, opposed without being contrary, the will of man and divine Providence. The infinite fractions of my being, which, in the future and by generation, will constitute, outside of you, the mass of humanity, would have been divided into two classes: the first emanating from thee, composed of volitive men, and the second emanating from thy brother, composed of providential men. These two classes of men, in elaborating one the other, lending each other mutual strength and enlightenment, would quite rapidly have led man to the perfection toward which he must tend, and reconstruct the edifice of knowledge to which immortality will be attached.

"This division, simple and easy to grasp, would have produced great advantages, which the new and more complicated division to be established will render more difficult to obtain. It would also have averted a great number of catastrophes and revolutions to which I foresee humanity will be exposed.

"In filling thee with a guilty intoxication, in depriving me of a son by thy hand, *Nahash* flattered himself that he was drying up the source of providential men, and destroying in Abel one of the two great powers that must rule the universe. Alone with thee and thy descendants, he hoped to subjugate you easily; and by your means, attain to the universal domination to which he aspires. But these things will not go according to his desires. Instead of two powers, as there would have been, there will be three. Thus the obstacles will multiply around him. They would be multiplied even more, if he succeeded, which is against all probability, in destroying another of them.

"Hear me with attention in order to comprehend well what will happen. The Eternal God, who has already received Abel into His bosom, prepares to return him to me, but stronger, and invested with a formidable power, which, without thy crime, would not have appeared in this world.

A son will be born to me in place of Abel, and because of his disappearance. He will be called Seth. In him will destiny be manifested, in the same manner as the will is manifest in thee. His descendants will be fatidical men, that is to say, men ordained to the fatality of destiny, as thine will be volitive men ordained to the will.

"By intermingling, sometimes conquering, sometimes conquered, they will oppose necessity to liberty, and liberty to necessity. Instead of the easy and ever voluntary yoke that thou wouldst have received from Abel, and that thy descendants would have received from his, you will often be burdened with a stiff yoke, which you will try in vain to break. The more you make efforts to throw it off, the more it will weigh upon you. When after a thousand trials you believe to be delivered from it under one form, it will reappear under another. Then you will regret Abel and the gentleness of his empire. You will call Providence to your help. But the descendants of Abel, the pure providential men, will not be among you.

"Providence, which would have been manifested immediately if Abel had lived, will be manifested only mediately; that is to say, either under the form of destiny, among fatidical men, or under the form of the will, among volitive men. This Supreme Power, the first of the three, will remain constantly veiled for you. You will feel, directly, only the action of the two others, the names of which you will change according to the circumstances: calling Providence that which is destiny or will; calling destiny or will that which is Providence.

"This is what the new division to be established will be.

Instead of two actions you will experience three; you would experience six, if a new shock took place in nature.   Depart, Cain.   Strive to reflect upon all that I have told thee; and may the Providence of the Eternal God guide thy steps in the course thou hast too unfortunately opened!''

END OF THE REMARKS